"An enlightening and edifying look at the most important week in history. Both those who want to know more about the history and those who long to behold the wonder will find much to love about this great work. One gets the sense that we should proceed through these pages on our knees."

J. D. Greear, lead pastor, The Summit Church, Durham, North Carolina; author, *Gospel* and *Stop Asking Jesus into Your Heart*

"You may be wondering what can be done to make Christ's last week come alive in ways it hasn't before. It would help to understand the historical background and cultural script a little better, but you don't want a big book. It would help, too, if your authors were trustworthy, knowledgeable evangelical scholars who could write clearly for laypeople. Look no further—this is the book for you!"

Craig L. Blomberg, distinguished professor of New Testament, Denver Seminary

"Whether you're a Christian seeking to defend your faith, an inquirer wanting to know what really happened with Jesus, or a disciple who wants to know the Lord more fully, *The Final Days of Jesus* will instruct and encourage you. It lays out the truth with coherence and conviction. I will point people to this book because it so clearly and faithfully explains what happened in the final days of Jesus. Here is the truth, based on the Gospel accounts. Here is the center of the Christian story, filled with insight and inspiration."

Mark D. Roberts, executive director, Max De Pree Center for Leadership, Fuller Theological Seminary; author, *Can We Trust the Gospels?*

"This is an immensely helpful guide to the last week of Jesus's life—historically, theologically, and devotionally. Historically, it provides a likely chronology of Passion Week, chock full of historical, cultural, and geographical insights. Theologically, the authors provide the text of the four Gospels with helpful commentary, noting the theological contributions of each evangelist. Devotionally, the reader has the privilege of walking with Jesus through the most important week of human history—the climax of God's redemptive plan. A feast of insights for both mind and heart."

Mark L. Strauss, professor of New Testament, Bethel Seminary San Diego

"Jesus's last week shook but also saved the world. From Palm Sunday to Easter morning, each day and encounter were critical. This book leads the reader step-by-step along Jesus's route from triumphal entry to the cross and finally to glory. Numerous maps and diagrams shed fresh light on each Gospel's claims. We are reminded not only of what Christ did but also where his way points us now. An excellent beginning-to-intermediate guide!"

Robert W. Yarbrough, professor of New Testament, Covenant Theological Seminary

"Holy Week is arguably the most sacred time of year for Christians. Andreas Köstenberger and Justin Taylor provide a simple yet eloquent survey of the final week of Jesus's life. They take readers on a pilgrimage through the Gospels and invite us to follow Jesus in his triumphal entry into Jerusalem, on to the dark and tragic moments of Golgotha, and through to the glorious and unspeakable joy at the feet of the risen Jesus. In short, this is a wonderful resource for individuals, families, and fellowships to learn more about the Easter story, the greatest story ever told."

Michael F. Bird, lecturer in theology, Ridley Melbourne College of Mission and Ministry

"A clearly presented overview of the most important week in world history. Brief, helpful comments illuminate the biblical story and bring home its enduring and life-changing message."

Douglas J. Moo, Kenneth T. Wessner Professor of New Testament, Wheaton College

"*The Final Days of Jesus* helps believers take note of the historical events leading up to Jesus's death on the cross. Readers are challenged to see the provocation that Jesus's message and life represented, leading to his arrest and execution. The book demonstrates that historical facts and Christian worship can and should go hand in hand."

Eckhard J. Schnabel, Mary F. Rockefeller Distinguished Professor of New Testament, Gordon-Conwell Theological Seminary

"The center point of history is the death and resurrection of Jesus Christ, the Son of God. Thus *The Final Days of Jesus* is an incredibly important work, for it enables us to see the full impact of the social and religious tension that lay behind Jesus's death as well as the theological implications for us. This book is both well researched and well written and is must-reading for students of the Word and indeed for all who wish to understand more fully the God-led events that resulted in the cross."

Grant Osborne, professor emeritus of New Testament, Trinity Evangelical Divinity School

"Ninety-eight percent of the students entering a particular Christian college last year claimed to be Christians. Yet twenty-five percent did not know that Christianity affirms that Jesus literally rose from the dead! What better way to rediscover this truth than to walk alongside the Savior during his final days and moments? Köstenberger and Taylor guide us on our pilgrimage, and they are outstanding guides. More than anything else, they remind us that Jesus final days are not really the end."

Charles L. Quarles, professor of New Testament and biblical theology, Southeastern Baptist Theological Seminary

TRUTH FOR LIFE®

THE BIBLE-TEACHING MINISTRY OF **ALISTAIR BEGG**

The mission of Truth For Life is to teach the Bible with clarity and relevance so that unbelievers will be converted, believers will be established, and local churches will be strengthened.

Daily Program

Each day, Truth For Life distributes the Bible teaching of Alistair Begg across the U.S., and in several locations outside of the U.S. on over 1,600 radio outlets. To find a radio station near you, visit **truthforlife.org/station-finder.**

Free Teaching

The daily program, and Truth For Life's entire teaching archive of over 2,000 Bible-teaching messages, can be accessed for free online and through Truth For Life's full-feature mobile app. A daily app is also available that provides direct access to the daily message and daily devotional. Download the free mobile apps at **truthforlife.org/app** and listen free online at **truthforlife.org.**

At-Cost Resources

Books and full-length teaching from Alistair Begg on CD, DVD and MP3CD are available for purchase at cost, with no mark up. Visit **truthforlife.org/store**.

Where To Begin?

If you're new to Truth For Life and would like to know where to begin listening and learning, find starting point suggestions at **truthforlife.org/firststep**. For a full list of ways to connect with Truth For Life, visit **truthforlife.org/subscribe.**

Contact Truth For Life

P.O. Box 398000 Cleveland, Ohio 44139
phone 1 (888) 588-7884   **email** letters@truthforlife.org
 /truthforlife @truthforlife **truthforlife.org**

THE·FINAL DAYS·OF JESUS

THE MOST IMPORTANT WEEK OF THE MOST IMPORTANT PERSON WHO EVER LIVED

ANDREAS J. KÖSTENBERGER
& JUSTIN TAYLOR
WITH ALEXANDER STEWART

WHEATON, ILLINOIS

The Final Days of Jesus: The Most Important Week of the Most Important Person Who Ever Lived
Copyright © 2014 by Andreas J. Köstenberger and Justin Taylor
Published by Crossway
       1300 Crescent Street
       Wheaton, Illinois 60187

Maps and illustrations are adapted from the ESV® Study Bible (The Holy Bible, English Standard Version®), copyright © 2008 by Crossway, a publishing ministry of Good News Publishers. Used by permission. All rights reserved.

Cover designer and illustrator: Adam Greene

First printing 2014

Printed in the United States of America

Scripture quotations are from the ESV® Bible (The Holy Bible, English Standard Version®), copyright © 2001 by Crossway, a publishing ministry of Good News Publishers. 2011 Text Edition. Used by permission. All rights reserved.

All emphases in Scripture quotations have been added by the authors.

Trade paperback ISBN: 978-1-4335-3510-9
ePub ISBN: 978-1-4335-3513-0
PDF ISBN: 978-1-4335-3511-6
Mobipocket ISBN: 978-1-4335-3512-3

Library of Congress Cataloging-in-Publication Data
Köstenberger, Andreas J., 1957–
   The final days of Jesus : the most important week of
the most important person who ever lived / Andreas J.
Köstenberger and Justin Taylor, with Alexander Stewart.
     pages cm
   Includes bibliographical references and index.
   ISBN 978-1-4335-3510-9 (tp)
   1. Jesus Christ—Passion—Devotional literature. I. Title.
BT431.3.K67   2014
232.96—dc23   2013027234

Crossway is a publishing ministry of Good News Publishers.

VP		28	27	26	25	24	23	22	21	20	19	18
17	16	15	14	13	12	11	10	9	8	7	6	5

To the crucified and risen Savior, who is our salvation

"I glorified you on earth,
having accomplished the work
that you gave me to do."
(John 17:4)

"It is finished."
(John 19:30)

Hallelujah!

CONTENTS

LIST OF CHARTS, DIAGRAMS, AND MAPS

Insert

INTRODUCTION

HOW TO USE THIS BOOK

The four Gospels contain eyewitness accounts (and first-hand reports) of the life, death, and resurrection of Jesus.

Jesus was born of a young virgin in the town of Bethlehem, perhaps in October of 6 or 5 BC.[1] After his mother, Mary, and his adoptive father, Joseph, fled to Egypt on account of the murderous designs of Herod the Great, the family relocated to the town of Nazareth in lower Galilee, where Joseph served as a carpenter. Apart from a brief account of Jesus's interaction with the rulers of Jerusalem when he was twelve years old (probably in AD 7 or 8), we hear no further details about the life of Jesus until the beginning of his public ministry, which likely began in late AD 29 and continued until his death on Friday, April 3, AD 33.[2]

Jesus's relatively brief public ministry began with his baptism and wilderness temptations, continued with his authoritative teaching and miracle-working power, and culminated in his atoning death at the hands of the Romans and Jews, followed by his resurrection and ascension.

This book covers Jesus's final days. In these pages you will read the eyewitness accounts of what the most important person who ever lived said and did during the most important week of his life. Sunday through Sunday—from what we now call "Palm Sunday" to "Easter Sunday"—we will put the accounts together in roughly

[1] Scholars usually suggest a date of 7–5 BC for Jesus's birth.
[2] Though note that many (if not most) date Jesus's death to AD 30. For more on this, see chapter 1, note 1.

chronological order, letting you read all four records of these events as we seek to explain to the best of our ability what is happening.

Before we proceed, it may be helpful to review some of the basics in order to set the stage and to remember the context of the four Gospels.

Who Wrote the Gospels?

Though the information has been doubted, there is good reason to believe that the Gospels were written by four men who were in the best possible position to recount what Jesus said and did.

Matthew and John, the authors of the first and fourth biblical Gospels, respectively, were members of the Twelve; John was even part of Jesus's inner circle (together with Peter and James).

Mark, the church fathers tell us, wrote his Gospel in close association with the apostle Peter, also one of the Twelve and a member of Jesus's inner circle as well as the preeminent spokesman of the Twelve.

Luke, finally, while not himself an eyewitness, sought to conduct a careful investigation of these events and acknowledges his dependence on "those who from the beginning were eyewitnesses and ministers of the word" (Luke 1:2). (The word he uses for "eyewitnesses" is *autoptēs*, a composite of two Greek words meaning "to see for oneself.")

As John writes in his first epistle,

That which was from the beginning,
    which we have heard,
    which we have seen with our eyes,
    which we looked upon
    and have touched with our hands,
concerning the word of life . . .
that which we have seen and heard
    we proclaim also to you,
so that you too may have fellowship with us. . . .
    And we are writing these things so that our joy may be
        complete. (1 John 1:1–4)

The result is that those of us today—reading the accounts two thousand years later—share an experience expressed by Peter:

> Though you have not seen him, you love him. Though you do not now see him, you believe in him and rejoice with joy that is inexpressible and filled with glory, obtaining the outcome of your faith, the salvation of your souls. (1 Pet. 1:8–9)

Why Were the Gospels Written?

As eyewitness accounts of the events surrounding Jesus's first coming, the four canonical Gospels demand our utmost attention. Why were they written? John says it most clearly:

> Now Jesus did many other signs in the presence of the disciples, which are not written in this book; but these are written so that you may believe that Jesus is the Christ, the Son of God, and that by believing you may have life in his name. (John 20:30–31)

Jesus is the Messiah, the Son of God—he is the promised, long-awaited Servant of the Lord who came to save us from our sin so that by believing we may have "life in his name."

Underneath this united, overarching purpose, we can recognize that the four Gospel authors wrote four complementary accounts designed for four distinct audiences. They used theological and literary selection in order to highlight certain aspects of Jesus's ministry, each painting a true and faithful portrait of the one Messiah.[3]

The tax-collector-turned-disciple *Matthew* (Levi), writing to a Jewish audience in the 50s or 60s, emphasizes Jesus as the Jewish Messiah predicted in the Old Testament, the son of David who comes to establish the kingdom of heaven.[4]

Peter's "interpreter" John *Mark*, writing to Gentiles in Rome in the mid- to late 50s, shows Jesus as the authoritative, suffering son of God who gives his life as a ransom for many.

---

[3] The following dates are approximations, and other scholars may date Matthew, Mark, and Luke later than is proposed here. Very few would date John earlier.
[4] The date for Matthew depends in part on whether one takes the position that Matthew wrote his Gospel first (Matthean priority) or that Mark was the first Gospel to be written (Markan priority).

Luke, a Gentile physician and travel companion to Paul, was writing a two-volume work around 58–60 to give an account of the truth of the faith to a man named Theophilus (who may also have paid for the publication of Luke–Acts), showing that Jesus is the savior of the world who seeks and saves the lost in fulfillment of the Old Testament promises to Israel.[5]

John, the beloved disciple of Jesus, was probably an old man when he composed his account in the mid- or late 80s or early 90s, written to the church in Ephesus to demonstrate that Jesus is the messiah who demands belief and the lamb of God who dies for the sins of the world and gives those who believe eternal life.

One of the more interesting differences between the Gospels is the strategy used to begin their biographies of Jesus's life and work. The Synoptics (Matthew, Mark, and Luke) begin *in history*, first recounting either the announcement of the birth of Jesus or the announcement of his prophetic forerunner John the Baptist. John, on the other hand, begins *before* history, *in heaven*, emphasizing the eternal relationship between God the Father and God the Son before the Son took on human nature. This is one of the reasons that the Synoptics are marked by greater similarity and overlap, whereas John often highlights other aspects of Jesus's ministry as part of his overall strategy.

But the question still remains: Would it not have been easier simply to provide one authoritative account of Jesus's life rather than four versions that at times don't harmonize very easily?

The answer is, first of all, that the early church did not consider our four Gospels as four *separate* Gospels but as *one* Gospel *according to* four different *witnesses*—the Gospel (singular) according to Matthew, Mark, Luke, and John. The early church had it right: there is only *one* gospel message (not four!), but for reasons of his

---

[5] The New Testament writers refer to the Old Testament in a variety of ways. Most widely known is the pattern of fulfillment-prediction, which highlights the fulfillment of messianic prophecy in Christ (e.g., Matt. 1:22–23 citing Isa. 7:14). But there are other ways the New Testament refers to the Old Testament as well, most notably typology. Typology involves an escalating salvation-historical pattern culminating in Christ (e.g., the serpent in the wilderness: John 3:14 citing Num. 21:9). In addition, the New Testament authors refer to the Old Testament by way of analogy, illustration, and commentary (*midrash* or *pesher*).

own God chose to provide us with four (rather than just one) eyewitness accounts of this one gospel.

Second, remember what we said earlier about the nature of the Gospels as eyewitness testimony. Like witnesses in the courtroom each recounting what they saw, using their own words and recalling events and statements from their unique perspective, the Gospel writers each tell us how *they* witnessed the unfolding story of Jesus (or in Mark's and Luke's case, how their firsthand sources did). This should in fact *enhance* our appreciation for the four biblical Gospels, not *diminish* it! Demonstrably, the four evangelists did not sanitize their accounts or somehow streamline them so as to make them artificially cohere; they were unafraid to tell the story of Jesus each in his own way, without fear of contradiction—because they were all witnessing to the *one* story of Jesus, the *one* gospel of our Lord Jesus Christ. Remember also that when the Gospels were written and published, there were still plenty of eyewitnesses around who could easily have disputed the veracity of the Gospel accounts—but we are not aware of any such challenges. For this reason we have every confidence that the one Gospel according to Matthew, Mark, Luke, and John is reliable.

Did It Really Happen?

Our primary response to the Gospels is not to criticize or to find fault but to believe. As we celebrate Easter, we can do so with a grateful heart and with the assurance that the Easter story is true—historically *and* theologically. Even though the primary design of the Gospels is for us to believe in this Messiah and to become his disciples, this does not mean it is illegitimate to explore the Gospel accounts intelligently. As Augustine and others after him have rightly asserted, faith of necessity seeks greater understanding. Our faith and our intellect should never be separated, as if (as some detractors allege) we were called to throw away our minds at conversion and blindly believe contrary to the evidence.

Critical scholars, with limited success, have sought to establish criteria for assessing the historicity of various teachings and events in the Gospels. One such criterion is the *criterion of multiple attestation*, according to which Gospel material is likely authentic if it is found in two or more Gospels or other ancient sources that are not dependent on each other. While it is widely held that Matthew, Mark, and Luke are in some way interrelated, John's account may classify as an independent witness to many of the same events as those recorded in the so-called Synoptic Gospels (i.e., Matthew, Mark, and Luke). This would underscore the likely historicity of these events using the criterion of multiple attestation.

Another criterion is *the criterion of dissimilarity*, according to which Gospel material is likely authentic if Jesus's teachings or actions differed from first-century Judaism or the practice of the early church. The early church, so the argument goes, would hardly have fabricated material that embarrassed the first Christians or weakened their stance in interaction with Christianity's detractors. Instead, embarrassing facts would likely have been omitted from the Gospel accounts. The fact, however, is that the Gospels include many such data that did not present Christianity in a favorable light—the apostles' rivalry and jockeying for position in Jesus's kingdom, their desertion of Jesus at his arrest, Peter's denials, and particularly the crucifixion itself, all at first glance seem to constitute embarrassing information that the church would likely have suppressed—unless these data are historical and the evangelists were honest enough to preserve them *despite* the fact that they were less than complimentary and do not present their own actions or people's response to Jesus in a positive light.

However, while these and other criteria are of some value in establishing positively the historicity of certain events recounted in the Gospels, they fall short in many ways, especially when critical scholars are trying to use these criteria negatively in order to disprove the authenticity of these accounts.

Two Ways to Read the Gospels

This, of course, does not remove the need for careful harmonization, that is, reading the four Gospels in tandem and trying to explain any apparent differences in detail of their presentation of individual statements or events. There are two—complementary and equally legitimate—ways of reading the Gospels.

The first is to read the Gospels *vertically*, that is, to read each account from beginning to end as a self-contained story in its own right. Matthew, Mark, Luke, and John each told their *own* story, and we must respect the literary and theological integrity of their work. This has been increasingly realized in recent years and underscores the importance of using (initially) Matthew to explain Matthew, Mark to explain Mark, and so forth.

The other way to read the Gospels is *horizontally*, that is, how each relates to the others, as complementary accounts and witnesses to the *same* historical reality and set of statements and events. Refusing to supplement our vertical reading of the individual Gospels with a horizontal reading is tantamount to the ostrich policy of refusing to acknowledge that while the Gospels *tell the same story*, they don't do so *in exactly the same way*.

Are There Contradictions?

As you work your way through this book, you will find many instances where we acknowledge differences among the Gospel accounts of individual details and make an honest attempt to suggest plausible ways in which those accounts may in fact cohere. As John writes at the conclusion of his Gospel, "Now there are also many other things that Jesus did. Were every one of them to be written, I suppose that the world itself could not contain the books that would be written" (John 21:25). This speaks to the inevitable *selectivity* at work in the Gospels. For this reason we must not assume that just because an evangelist does not *mention* a given detail, he was necessarily unaware of it or would have disputed its accuracy. Furthermore, we must be careful not to read these accounts anachronistically, imposing artificial limitations or requiring unreasonable precision upon eyewitness testimony and the genre of ancient theological biography. A simple example can be illustrated in what was written on the epitaph of the cross above Jesus's crucified head. Each Gospel writer gives us a slightly different version:

Jesus's Crucifixion Epitaph: Differences in Wording

Jesus of Nazareth, the King of the Jews		John 19:19
This is Jesus,	the King of the Jews	Matt. 27:37
	the King of the Jews	Mark 15:26
This is	the King of the Jews	Luke 23:38

A charitable rather than critical reading clearly demonstrates that the evangelists are each accurately referring to the same thing rather than contradicting one another. This is consistent with the way that true (rather than artificial or deceptive) eyewitness testimony takes place: different observers remember and choose to highlight different aspects of the one event.

So we ought to read the Gospels sympathetically, giving them the benefit of the doubt, rather than reading between the lines critically, looking for problems. The burden of proof lies on those who would convict the Gospels of incoherence, not on the Gospels to prove their integrity!

Using This Book

How, then, do we recommend that you use this book? Essentially, we provide you with an account of Jesus's final week from Palm Sunday through Easter Sunday, with brief presentations of preceding and subsequent events in a prologue and epilogue.

Beginning with Wednesday of the final week, we have included the complete text of Scripture for this time period, with the intention that you will first read and meditate upon God's authoritative Word and only then read our attempts to comment on what you have read.

We envision that churches, families, small groups, and individuals will benefit from reading through the biblical material and accompanying commentary in sequence on each day of Holy Week, though certainly this subject is worthy of meditation throughout the year. Naturally, some days contain less material than others; Good Friday is particularly lengthy, so it would be good for you to plan on setting aside additional time to work through the material. The study could culminate in a special sermon, lesson, or study on Easter Sunday, including reflection on the significance of Easter and Jesus's resurrection.

While the primary purpose of this book is not academic—instead, our desire is to provide an aid to informed worship—and we have thus refrained from providing extensive references to the scholarly literature, the discussion is informed by responsible evangelical scholarship. There is a rich tapestry of historical detail, literary artistry, and theological insight to be gleaned from the Gospel accounts of Jesus's final week, and we have done our best to include all the relevant material and to do so in a way that is informative, intelligible, and interesting to read.

For those who are interested in doing further study of the Gospel presentation of Jesus's final week, we have provided a list of suggested resources. We have also included a glossary that provides brief sketches of the most important characters in the Gospel story as well as geographical and topographical information and other important data. Before you delve into your study, it will also be helpful to familiarize yourself with the sequence of events as presented in the immediately following Scripture Guide to the Events of Holy Week.

It is our prayer that God will see fit to use this volume to bring glory to himself and to the Lord Jesus Christ. "For I [Paul] delivered to you as of first importance what I also received: that Christ died for our sins in accordance with the Scriptures, that he was buried, that he was raised on the third day in accordance with the Scriptures, and that he appeared to Cephas [Peter], then to the twelve" (1 Cor. 15:3–5). *Soli Deo gloria*—to God alone be the glory!

SCRIPTURE GUIDE TO THE EVENTS OF HOLY WEEK

Sunday

Jesus enters Jerusalem	Matt. 21:1-11; Mark 11:1-10; Luke 19:29-44; John 12:12-19
Jesus predicts his death	John 12:20-36
Jesus visits the temple	Matt. 21:14-17; Mark 11:11

Monday

Jesus curses a fig tree	Matt. 21:18-19; Mark 11:12-14
Jesus cleanses the temple	Matt. 21:12-13; Mark 11:15-18; Luke 19:45-48

Tuesday

The lesson from the fig tree	Matt. 21:20-22; Mark 11:20-26
Jesus teaches and engages in controversies in the temple	Matt. 21:23-23:39; Mark 11:27-12:44; Luke 20:1-21:4
Jesus predicts the future	Matt. 24-25; Mark 13:1-37; Luke 21:5-36

Wednesday[1]

Jesus continues his daily teaching in the temple complex	Luke 21:37-38

---

[1] We don't really know for sure that either of these events occurred on Wednesday. This is just one possible option.

The Sanhedrin plots to kill Jesus	Matt. 26:3-5; Mark 14:1-2; Luke 22:1-2

Thursday

Jesus instructs his disciples Peter and John to secure a large upper room in a house in Jerusalem and to prepare for the Passover meal	Matt. 26:17-19; Mark 14:12-16; Luke 22:7-13
In the evening Jesus eats the Passover meal with the Twelve, tells them of the coming betrayal, and institutes the Lord's Supper	Matt. 26:20-29; Mark 14:17-23; Luke 22:14-30
During supper Jesus washes the disciples' feet, interacts with them, and delivers the Upper Room Discourse (Farewell Discourse)	John 13:1-17:26
Jesus and the disciples sing a hymn together, then depart to the Mount of Olives	Matt. 26:30; Mark 14:26; Luke 22:39
Jesus predicts Peter's denials	Matt. 26:31-35; Mark 14:27-31; Luke 22:31-34
Jesus issues final practical commands about supplies and provisions	Luke 22:35-38
Jesus and the disciples go to Gethsemane, where he struggles in prayer and they struggle to stay awake late into the night	Matt. 26:36-46; Mark 14:32-42; Luke 22:40-46

Friday

Jesus is betrayed by Judas and arrested by the authorities (perhaps after midnight, early Friday morning)	Matt. 26:47-56; Mark 14:43-52; Luke 22:47-53; John 18:2-12

Jesus has an informal hearing before Annas (former high priest and Caiaphas's father-in-law)	Matt. 26:57, 59-68; Mark 14:53, 55-65; Luke 22:63-71
As predicted, Peter denies Jesus and the rooster crows	Matt. 26:58, 69-75; Mark 14:54, 66-72; Luke 22:54b-62; John 18:15-18, 25-27
After sunrise on Friday the final consultation of the full Sanhedrin condemns Jesus to death and sends him to Pontius Pilate	Matt. 27:1-2; Mark 15:1
Judas changes his mind, returns the silver, and hangs himself	Matt. 27:3-10
Pilate questions Jesus and sends him to Herod Antipas	Matt. 27:11-14; Mark 15:2-5; Luke 23:1-7; John 18:28-38
Herod questions Jesus and sends him back to Pilate	Luke 23:8-12
Jesus appears before Pilate a second time and is condemned to die	Matt. 27:15-26; Mark 15:6-15; Luke 23:13-25; John 18:38b-19:16
Jesus is mocked and marched to Golgotha	Matt. 27:27-34; Mark 15:16-23; Luke 23:26-49; John 19:17
Jesus is crucified between two thieves	Matt. 27:35-44; Mark 15:24-32; Luke 23:33-43; John 19:18-27
Jesus breathes his last	Matt. 27:45-56; Mark 15:33-41; Luke 23:44-49; John 19:28-37
Joseph of Arimathea buries Jesus in a new tomb	Matt. 27:57-61; Mark 15:42-47; Luke 23:50-56; John 19:38-42

Saturday

The chief priests and Pharisees place guards at the tomb with Pilate's permission	Matt. 27:62-66

Sunday

Some women discover the empty tomb and are instructed by angels	Matt. 28:1-7; Mark 16:1-7; Luke 24:1-7; John 20:1
The women, fearful and joyful, leave the garden and tell the disciples	Matt. 28:8-10; Luke 24:8-11; John 20:2
Peter and John rush to the tomb based upon Mary Magdalene's report and discover it empty	Luke 24:12; John 20:3-10
Mary returns to the tomb and encounters Jesus	John 20:11-18
Jesus appears to Cleopas and a friend on the road to Emmaus	Luke 24:13-35
That evening Jesus appears to the Eleven (minus Thomas) in a house in Jerusalem	Luke 24:36-43; John 20:19-23

Later Appearances of Jesus and the Ascension

Jesus appears to the Eleven (including Thomas)	John 20:24-31
Jesus appears to some at the Sea of Galilee	John 21
The Great Commission	Matt. 28:16-20 (see also Luke 24:45-49; John 20:21-23; Acts 1:8)
The ascension	Luke 24:50-53; Acts 1:9-11

EARLY IN THE WEEK

THE KING COMES FOR HIS KINGDOM

SUNDAY–TUESDAY

The year was AD 33.[1] The excitement in the cool spring air of Jerusalem was palpable. Thousands of Jewish pilgrims had gathered
from around the world for the upcoming Passover feast, and word
had spread that Jesus—a thirty-something itinerant rabbi, prophet,
and healer from Galilee—had raised Lazarus from the dead, had
withdrawn from Bethany—a village just a couple miles east of Jerusalem—to a town called Ephraim in the wilderness (John 11:54),
and was staying at Bethany during the weekend prior to Passover
(John 11:55–12:1, 9–11).[2] Many had gone to Bethany to see Jesus
and Lazarus, with the result that they believed in Jesus and returned
to the capital city with reports of his miracle-working power to
raise the dead (John 12:9–11, 17–18). The Passover crowds in Jerusalem were like a powder keg ready for a spark—filled to the brim
with both messianic fervor and hatred of Roman rule.

Winds of revolution whipped through the air of Palestine
throughout the first century, and Jesus, with his teaching author-

---

[1] Most scholars believe that Jesus was crucified in AD 30. We are persuaded that the evidence
strongly points to a date of AD 33. For an introductory discussion of the issues, see Andreas J.
Köstenberger, "The Date of Jesus' Crucifixion," *ESV Study Bible*, ed. Wayne Grudem (Wheaton, IL:
Crossway, 2008), 1809–10. See also Colin J. Humphreys and W. G. Waddington, "The Jewish Calendar, A Lunar Eclipse and the Date of Christ's Crucifixion," *Tyndale Bulletin* 43.2 (1992): 331–51.
[2] Many Jews came to Jerusalem a week early to ceremonially cleanse themselves and prepare
for the Passover.

ity and ability to capture the imagination of the masses, not least on account of his ability to heal and raise the dead, looked very much the part of the long-awaited Messiah. In order to gain and maintain power, the Romans could kill—which they did quite effectively—but how could they defeat a leader who could raise the dead at will?

After observing the Sabbath (Friday evening through Saturday evening) at Bethany, Jesus arose Sunday morning to enter the city of Jerusalem. It was March 29, AD 33—the first day of the last week of his earthly life.

SUNDAY

MARCH 29, AD 33

Jesus Enters Jerusalem
(Matt. 21:1-11; Mark 11:1-10; Luke 19:29-44; John 12:12-19)

The Passover crowds and inhabitants of Jerusalem were filled with messianic expectation, and Jesus does not disappoint. On Sunday morning, Jesus and his disciples are on the Mount of Olives as they approach Jerusalem. He sends two of his followers to the nearby village (Bethphage or Bethany), instructing them to bring a donkey and colt on which he will sit for his entrance into Jerusalem. By this intentional symbolic action, Jesus will clearly communicate his kingship to the expectant crowds of Passover pilgrims by fulfilling the prophecy of Zechariah 9:9, that Israel's future king would come riding on the foal of a donkey, and by copying Solomon's entrance into Jerusalem when he was declared king.[1]

As Jesus makes his westward descent down the Mount of Olives and toward the Holy City, the crowds rightly interpret his actions with expectant joy and respond in kind by spreading robes and leafy palm branches in his pathway to create a royal red carpet (see 2 Kings 9:13) and by acclaiming him their Davidic king:

---

[1] 1 Kings 1:32–40. Matthew makes mention of two animals, a colt (the animal that would have carried Jesus) and a donkey (presumably the colt's mother; Matt. 21:7). Mark and Luke both mention only the colt and note that no one had ever ridden it before (Mark 11:2; Luke 19:30), hence perhaps the need for the colt's mother to steady it as it carried its first rider.

> Hosanna to the Son of David!
> Blessed is he who comes in the name of the Lord!
>> Hosanna in the highest!
> Blessed is the coming kingdom of our father David!
>> (Matt. 21:9; Mark 11:10; see also Isa. 9:7)

The crowds are openly acclaiming Jesus instead of Caesar as king!

The whole city is shaken by the events, and the crowd keeps spreading the word to any in Jerusalem who have not yet heard who Jesus is (Matt. 21:10–11). Some Pharisees instruct Jesus to rebuke the crowds for their dangerous messianic exuberance, but he refuses to correct or curtail the excitement of the crowd over his entrance into the city (Matt. 21:15–17; Luke 19:39–40). It would be hard to overestimate the political and religious volatility incited by Jesus's actions—the Pharisees were taken by surprise and had no idea how to respond (John 12:19). Up to this point in Jesus's ministry, he could still have managed to live a long, happy, peaceful life, but his actions on Sunday set in motion a series of events that could result only in either his overthrow of the Romans and the current religious establishment—or his brutal death. He has crossed the point of no return; there would be no turning back. Caesar could allow no rival kings. As Jesus approaches the city, he weeps over Jerusalem (Luke 19:41–44).

Jesus Predicts His Death (John 12:20-36)

Some Greeks who were among the Passover pilgrims seek an audience with Jesus. John does not record the Greeks' question, but Jesus responds by predicting his death and describing it as the very purpose for which he has come into the world (John 12:27). A voice from heaven, thunderous in sound, affirms God's commitment to glorify his name through the coming death of Jesus (John 12:28–29). Jesus goes on to clarify the kind of fate he will meet: death by crucifixion (being "lifted up from the earth," John 12:32; see Isa. 52:13). Yet by his death, Jesus will deal Satan a crushing blow (John 12:31; see also Luke 10:18; Gen. 3:15).

The Jewish crowd, of course, does not like this kind of talk and objects that according to the Mosaic law, the Messiah must remain forever. Jesus does not directly answer their objection but instead commands them to "walk while [they] have the light" (i.e., Jesus himself, the "light of the world," John 8:12; 9:5) and believe in the light in order to become sons of light before it is gone and darkness comes (John 12:35–36).

Jesus Visits the Temple (Matt. 21:14-17; Mark 11:11)

Before returning with the Twelve to Bethany at the end of the day, Jesus visits the temple complex. Jesus continues to upset the religious establishment: healing the blind and lame, and receiving the praise of children.

This initial visit to the temple sets the stage for the unforgettable events that are to occur there the following day.

MONDAY

MARCH 30, AD 33

Jesus Curses a Fig Tree (Matt. 21:18-19; Mark 11:12-14)

As Jesus and his disciples are returning to Jerusalem Monday morning, Jesus, being hungry, spots a fig tree. Israel is often characterized as a fig tree in the Old Testament (Jer. 8:13; Hos. 9:10, 16; Joel 1:7), and Jesus's cursing of the fig tree symbolizes the judgment of God upon a nation that has the outward appearance of life but fails to bear fruit.

Jesus Cleanses the Temple
(Matt. 21:12-13; Mark 11:15-18; Luke 19:45-48)

With the riveting events of the previous day still fresh in everyone's mind, all eyes are on Jesus as he enters the city Monday morning. What will the recently hailed Davidic Messiah do to bring about his kingdom? Jesus wastes no time in answering this question by going straight to the temple.

From his visit the night before, he knows exactly what he will find there—moneychangers and merchants selling sacrificial animals in the Court of Gentiles. These profiteers prey upon the religious devotion of the Passover pilgrims who must pay the temple tax with a Tyrian shekel and present unblemished animals for sacrifice. Consumed by holy zeal and righteous indignation, Jesus overturns the tables and chairs of the moneychangers, throws out merchants and customers alike, and refuses entrance to any who are carrying goods for sale. He then begins to teach the people that the temple was to be a house of prayer for all nations (see Isa. 56:7; Jer. 7:11), not a den of thieves where the rich and powerful exploited the poor under the guise of facilitating worship of God.

By these actions, Jesus directly challenges the Jewish religious leadership complicit with—and likely benefiting from—this glaring corruption of devotion to Israel's covenant-keeping God. The chief priests, scribes, and leaders of the people desperately begin looking for a way to destroy Jesus. Not only had he directly challenged Jewish authority, but the Romans needed no excuse to exercise force if there was any civil instability. In contrast, the common people love what they are seeing. Jesus is shaking things up and setting things right just as the Messiah was expected to do. At the same time, however, by cleansing the temple Jesus further seals his death sentence. Those in power will not put up with a challenge to their authority on this level. Jesus must die.

When evening comes, Jesus and his followers leave Jerusalem once again (Mark 11:19; Luke 21:37).

TUESDAY

MARCH 31, AD 33

Jesus Teaches His Followers a Lesson about the Fig Tree
(Matt. 21:20-22; Mark 11:20-26)

When passing by the fig tree Jesus had cursed the day before, and at Peter's remark that it had withered, Jesus takes the opportunity to instruct his followers to have faith in God.[1] If they do not doubt but believe, they will be able to move spiritual mountains by way of believing prayer. While praying, they must forgive others who have wronged them, so that their own sins will be forgiven by God as well.

Jesus Teaches and Engages in Controversies in the Temple
(Matt. 21:23-23:39; Mark 11:27-12:44; Luke 20:1-21:4)

On Tuesday morning, the crowds come early to the temple to hear Jesus speak (Luke 21:38). Will Jesus do anything today to match the excitement of the previous two days?

The chief priests, scribes, and elders immediately approach Jesus when he enters the temple and confront him concerning his actions on the previous day: "By what authority are you doing these things, or who gave you this authority to do them?" (Mark 11:28). *They* are the ones who have authority over the temple and its activities, and Jesus had no right to do what he had done.

---

[1] Note that Matthew simply telescopes the events whereas Mark indicates that the cursing of the fig tree occurred on Monday while Jesus's instruction took place the following day.

Depending on his answer—and there was no answer that would satisfy them—Jesus could be arrested for his actions.

In reply, Jesus turns the tables on them by promising to answer their question if they first answer his: "Was the baptism of John from heaven or from man?" (Mark 11:30). The religious leaders are caught, unable to answer Jesus's simple question. If they were to say, "From heaven," the obvious follow-up would be, "Then why don't the leaders believe in Jesus about whom John testified?" If they were to retort, "From man," they would incur the wrath of the common people who hold John in high esteem as a prophet sent from God.

After thus humbling the Jewish leaders, Jesus follows up his question—the answer to which was in any case obvious to the crowds—with a series of parables. The parable of the two sons (Matt. 21:28–32) explicitly condemns the religious authorities for not believing John's message, while tax collectors and prostitutes, the most wicked kinds of people imaginable, believe and are entering the kingdom of God ahead of the supposed spiritual leaders. This parable must have infuriated the Jewish authorities, but Jesus adds fuel to the fire with two more parables directed against them.

In the parable of the tenants (Matt. 21:33–44; Mark 12:1–11; Luke 20:9–18), the disobedient, thieving, murdering tenants clearly represent the scribes, chief priests, and Pharisees. There is nothing subtle about Jesus's telling of the parable: the religious leaders recognize the parable as having been spoken against them (Matt. 21:45; Mark 12:12; Luke 20:19). The parable is allegorical with the following correspondences:

The Parable of the Tenants

PARABLE	REPRESENTATION
Vineyard owner	God
Vineyard	Israel
Slaves	God's prophets

PARABLE	REPRESENTATION
The son	Jesus
Destruction of the evil tenants	God's judgment on Israel's unrighteous leaders
Giving of the vineyard to others	Extension of God's kingdom to the Gentiles

In the parable of the wedding feast (Matt. 22:1–14), Jesus makes similar points. The current religious leadership have rejected God's invitation to the messianic wedding banquet and will be judged while the invitation is extended to all.

Jesus is clearly winning the support and approval of the people while exposing the failure and hypocrisy of the ruling Jewish leadership. The authorities, for their part, do not take this lying down and continue trying to figure out a way to arrest him; but they lack the opportunity because of Jesus's widespread popularity among the crowds (Matt. 21:46; 22:15; Mark 12:12–13; Luke 20:19–20). If they seize him, the attempted arrest would cause a riot. The leaders therefore resort to a subtler tactic and try to trick Jesus into incriminating himself by sending Pharisees (a Jewish sect known for its zeal to keep the law) and Herodians (those loyal to Herod's dynasty) to ask him a question to which either answer would provide grounds to accuse him: "Is it lawful to pay taxes to Caesar, or not?" (Matt. 22:15–22; Mark 12:13–17; Luke 20:20–26). If Jesus answers yes, he would shatter people's expectations of him as a Messiah who would throw off Roman rule; if no, he could be arrested for fomenting revolt. The temporary alliance of the Herodians and Pharisees (Jesus's political and religious adversaries) clearly demonstrated that Jesus was perceived as a threat to all the existing power structures. His clever answer avoids the trap by allowing for a both/and scenario, evading the either/or dilemma posed by his foes: the denarius has Caesar's image on it; so as long as Caesar is in power, it is appropriate to pay taxes to him (of course, in the messianic kingdom Caesar's image would not be on the coinage, so there the obligation would no longer apply). At the same time, Jesus urges his listeners to give God the things that are God's; since we are made in God's image, we owe everything to him. The image of Caesar and Roman gods on coins deeply offended Jews in the first century. Yet Jesus cleverly sidesteps their trap, and the Pharisees and Herodians, amazed at his answer, are at a loss as to how to respond.

After Jesus has silenced the Pharisees and Herodians, the Sadducees (a Jewish sect that denied the end-time resurrection of the dead) step forward to test him with a tricky theological conundrum (Matt. 22:23–33; Mark 12:18–27; Luke 20:27–40). Their question is designed to make Jesus's belief in the resurrection look ridiculous. But by quoting God's self-affirmation in Exodus 3:6, 15–16 to the effect that he is a God of the living, not the dead, Jesus once again turns the tables on his opponents.[2] They marvel at his answer and, as do the others who tried to trick him, fall silent.

Now another questioner, at the instigation of the Pharisees, steps forward in order to test Jesus (Matt. 22:34–35). An expert in the law asks Jesus which of God's commands is the greatest (Matt. 22:34–40; Mark 12:28–34). Jesus responds by quoting Deuteronomy 6:4–5 and Leviticus 19:18, calling for love of God and one's fellow man, and the following conversation leads Jesus to commend (and implicitly invite) the questioner: "You are not far from the kingdom of God" (Mark 12:34).

At this point, Jesus goes on the counteroffensive against those who have been trying to trap him and asks them a question concerning the way in which Psalm 110:1 describes the Messiah as David's Lord: How can he at once be both David's son and his Lord? (Matt. 22:41–46; Mark 12:35–37; Luke 20:41–44). Being of Davidic ancestry posed no problem for the Messiah's being Lord, but if this ancestry was interpreted as making him *merely human*, then there was a problem. Again, the opposition is utterly confounded:

---

[2]Jesus likely cited a passage from the Pentateuch because the Sadducees derived doctrine only from the five books of Moses.

"And no one was able to answer him a word, nor from that day did anyone dare to ask him any more questions" (Matt. 22:46).

Having established the inability of the Jewish religious leadership to answer Jesus's questions, Jesus launches a lengthy, scathing critique of the scribes and Pharisees (Matt. 23:1–39; Mark 12:38–40; Luke 20:45–47). He warns the crowds against those "hypocrites" and "blind guides" and pronounces seven woes of judgment against them. This full-scale verbal assault against the current religious authorities removes all doubt concerning Jesus's intentions, agenda, and aims. He has no desire to ally himself with the current leadership; he has come to overthrow their authority and to replace it with his own. There is no way that both sides can survive the escalating conflict. It seems that either Jesus will come to assume power or face death.

Jesus Predicts the Future
(Matthew 24-25; Mark 13:1-37; Luke 21:5-36)

As Jesus is leaving the temple on Tuesday evening, his disciples are discussing the size and grandeur of the buildings in the temple complex. In response, Jesus prophesies that the day is fast approaching when not one stone will be left upon another. All will be thrown down.

When Jesus and his disciples stop to rest on the Mount of Olives, his followers come to him and privately ask about the timing of his prophecy: "Tell us, when will these things be, and what will be the sign when all these things are about to be accomplished?" (Mark 13:4; Luke 21:7). "And what will be the sign of your coming and of the end of the age?" (Matt 24:3). The disciples' question in Mark and Luke relates to the timing of the destruction of the temple, while Matthew's inclusion of the question concerning the close of the age makes clear that the disciples did not think the temple would be destroyed until the end of time.

Jesus's lengthy response in Matthew, Mark, and Luke subtly differentiates the two events (though interpreters vary as to which event Jesus refers in the various parts of the discourse). It is not always clear whether Jesus is giving instructions to his disciples concerning the destruction of Jerusalem (which would take place in AD 70) or concerning his second coming and the end of the age (which was in the more distant future from the vantage point of Jesus's original followers and is still future from our vantage point today). In keeping with prophetic convention, the near event—the destruction of the temple—served as a type (picture or foreshadowing) of the worldwide divine judgment that will come upon the earth at Christ's return. The main themes of Jesus's discourse, reinforced by the parables of the ten virgins and of the talents, are clear. Followers of Jesus will experience increasing persecution and tribulation leading up to the final day of judgment, but they must remain vigilant and persist in faith.

Conclusion

With this overview of the early events of Passion Week in mind, we have a good foundation for our closer look at Jesus's final days. The stage is set for the final act. The characters are in place. Their goals, motives, and intentions are clear. The king has come for his kingdom and has issued a clear and direct challenge to the reigning structures of political, economic, and religious power. The drama can end in only one of two ways. Either Jesus will topple the reigning powers and establish his messianic kingdom—or he will be killed. No one at that time could possibly comprehend that in God's mysterious plan, there was a third option.

WEDNESDAY

THE PLOT AGAINST JESUS

Jesus continues his daily teaching in the temple complex.

LUKE 21:37-38

And every day he was teaching in the temple, but at night he went out and lodged on the mount called Olivet. And early in the morning all the people came to him in the temple to hear him.

The Sanhedrin plots to kill Jesus.

MATTHEW 26:3-5

Then the chief priests and the elders of the people gathered in the palace of the high priest, whose name was Caiaphas, and plotted together in order to arrest Jesus by stealth and kill him. But they said, "Not during the feast, lest there be an uproar among the people."

MARK 14:1-2

It was now two days before the Passover and the Feast of Unleavened Bread. And the chief priests and the scribes were seeking how to arrest him by stealth and kill him, for they said, "Not during the feast, lest there be an uproar from the people."

LUKE 22:1-2

Now the Feast of Unleavened Bread drew near, which is called the Passover. And the chief priests and the scribes were seeking how to put him to death, for they feared the people.

COMMENTARY

Jesus's Daily Teaching

Wednesday passes quietly—particularly when compared with the earlier city-shaking events of Sunday (the Triumphal Entry), Monday (the cleansing of the temple), and Tuesday (temple controversies). Jesus continues his daily practice of traveling from Bethany to Jerusalem early to teach the people in the temple complex. There do not seem to be any recorded controversies, but Luke notes the rapt attention of the crowds who had come to hear Jesus teach. His authority, actions, and teaching have made him quite a celebrity in the eyes of the people.

Not everyone is friendly, however. Jesus has a contingent of powerful and determined enemies.

The Plotting of the Sanhedrin

Matthew, Mark, and Luke each describe the murderous plotting of the chief priests, scribes, and elders of the people "two days before the Passover and the Feast of Unleavened Bread" (Mark 14:1). Matthew informs us that this meeting took place in the "palace" of Caiaphas the high priest (i.e., his private residence; Matt. 26:3).[1] This elite group of Jewish leaders is representative of the Sanhedrin (though the text does not indicate that the entire Sanhedrin met at this time). They gather to brainstorm a way to kill Jesus by stealth in order to avoid a major uproar among the masses. The general consensus is that they must wait until after the Feast of Unleavened Bread (a weeklong festival ending on Nisan 21 [Thursday, April 9]), when the crowds would disperse and return

---

[1] "Palace" may suggest a monarch's residence but in the present context refers to Caiaphas's home.

to their homes away from the city. At this point, they would be free to arrest and kill Jesus without fear of inciting a revolt. They are willing to bide their time because they know—or think they know—that they are in positions of power and authority and that if they wait for the right time to dispense with Jesus, they will win in the end.

Their mind is made up, and their verdict has been rendered.

THURSDAY

APRIL 2, AD 33

PREPARATIONS FOR THE PASSOVER

Jesus instructs his disciples Peter and John to secure a large upper room in a house in Jerusalem and to prepare for the Passover meal.

MATTHEW 26:17-19

Now on the first day of Unleavened Bread the disciples came to Jesus, saying,

"Where will you have us prepare for you to eat the Passover?"

He said,

"Go into the city to a certain man and say to him,

'The Teacher says, My time is at hand. I will keep the Passover at your house with my disciples.'"

And the disciples did as Jesus had directed them, and they prepared the Passover.

MARK 14:12-16

And on the first day of Unleavened Bread, when they sacrificed the Passover lamb, his disciples said to him,

"Where will you have us go and prepare for you to eat the Passover?"

And he sent two of his disciples and said to them,

"Go into the city, and a man carrying a jar of water will meet you. Follow him, and wherever he enters, say to the master of the house,

'The Teacher says,

> Where is my guest room, where I may eat the Passover with my disciples?'

And he will show you a large upper room furnished and ready; there prepare for us."

And the disciples set out and went to the city and found it just as he had told them, and they prepared the Passover.

LUKE 22:7-13

Then came the day of Unleavened Bread, on which the Passover lamb had to be sacrificed.

So Jesus sent Peter and John, saying,

"Go and prepare the Passover for us, that we may eat it."

They said to him,

"Where will you have us prepare it?"

He said to them,

"Behold, when you have entered the city, a man carrying a jar of water will meet you. Follow him into the house that he enters and tell the master of the house,

'The Teacher says to you,

> Where is the guest room, where I may eat the Passover with my disciples?'

And he will show you a large upper room furnished; prepare it there."

And they went and found it just as he had told them, and they prepared the Passover.

COMMENTARY

In Jewish reckoning, a new day began at nightfall, so Wednesday nightfall to Thursday nightfall (Nisan 14) was the day of preparation for the Passover meal. The Passover meal itself—including roasted lamb, bitter herbs, unleavened bread, fruit sauce, and four cups of wine—would have been shared after sundown that evening, Nisan 15 (Thursday nightfall to Friday nightfall).[1] In the original Passover, the blood of the lambs had been applied to the homes of the Israelites in Egypt to protect them from the outpouring of God's judgment upon the Egyptians (Ex. 12:7, 12–13, 22–28).[2]

Jesus's Final Days

April 2	Nisan 14	Thursday (Wednesday nightfall to Thursday nightfall)	Day of Passover preparation
April 3	Nisan 15	Friday (Thursday nightfall to Friday nightfall)	Passover; Feast of Unleavened Bread begins
April 4	Nisan 16	Saturday (Friday nightfall to Saturday nightfall)	Sabbath
April 5	Nisan 17	Sunday (Saturday nightfall to Sunday nightfall)	First day of the week

Matthew alone records Jesus telling his disciples, "My time is at hand," on the morning of the day on which the Passover lamb was sacrificed (Matt. 26:18). Jesus knows that he is about to die, but his disciples and the original hearers consistently fail to grasp the reality of Jesus's predictions. They likely understand his claim in light of their own version of messianic expectations: he is about to

---

[1] The references in John 13:1; 18:28; and 19:14 that seem to describe the Passover meal as yet to come do not present a genuine contradiction. The celebration of Passover and the seven-day Feast of Unleavened Bread were joined together in popular observance (see Matt. 26:17; Mark 14:12; Luke 22:1, 7), so the statements in John 18:28 and 19:14 likely represent the desire of the Jewish leaders to avoid defilement so that they could continue participating in the ongoing festival.
[2] The early Christians rightly interpreted Jesus's death as that of the ultimate Passover Lamb whose blood would shield his people from God's wrath against sinful humanity. Paul makes this exact point when he argues that "Christ, our Passover lamb, has been sacrificed" (1 Cor. 5:7).

force the ultimate confrontation that will lead to his victory over the Jewish religious leaders and the Roman overlords.[3] But Jesus means that the time is at hand for him to be sacrificed as God's Passover lamb in order to atone for the sins of the entire world.

According to Old Testament regulations (Deut. 16:5–6), the Passover must be eaten within the city of Jerusalem. Because of Jesus's celebrity status and the plot against him, his preparations for the Passover are conducted with a degree of secrecy. These preparations include the procurement, sacrifice, and roasting of a lamb along with the preparation of the room and side dishes. Jesus sends two of his disciples (Luke 22:8 mentions they were Peter and John) into the city to meet with an unnamed contact who will direct them to the room where they can eat the Passover. Most likely, Jesus had quietly made these arrangements ahead of time with supporters in the city. Since it was normally women who carried water jugs in that culture, the unusual sight of a man carrying such a jug suggests that it was likely a prearranged signal, and the man with the water jug was looking for the disciples. Peter and John find the arrangements exactly as Jesus had predicted.[4]

THE FINAL PASSOVER: THE SYNOPTICS

In the evening Jesus eats the Passover meal with the Twelve, tells them of the coming betrayal, and institutes the Lord's Supper.

MATTHEW 26:20-29

When it was evening, he reclined at table with the twelve. And as they were eating, he said,

"Truly, I say to you, one of you will betray me."

And they were very sorrowful and began to say to him one after another,

---

[3] Matthew 16:21; 17:22–23; 20:17–19; 26:2.
[4] Mark 14:16; Luke 22:13.

"Is it I, Lord?"

He answered,

"He who has dipped his hand in the dish with me will betray me.

The Son of Man goes as it is written of him, but woe to that man by whom the Son of Man is betrayed!

It would have been better for that man if he had not been born."

Judas, who would betray him, answered,

"Is it I, Rabbi?"

He said to him,

"You have said so."

Now as they were eating, Jesus took bread, and after blessing it broke it and gave it to the disciples, and said,

"Take, eat; this is my body."

And he took a cup, and when he had given thanks he gave it to them, saying,

"Drink of it, all of you, for this is my blood of the covenant, which is poured out for many for the forgiveness of sins.

I tell you I will not drink again of this fruit of the vine until that day when I drink it new with you in my Father's kingdom."

MARK 14:17-23

And when it was evening, he came with the twelve. And as they were reclining at table and eating, Jesus said,

"Truly, I say to you, one of you will betray me, one who is eating with me."

They began to be sorrowful and to say to him one after another,

"Is it I?"

He said to them,

> "It is one of the twelve, one who is dipping bread into the dish with me.
>
> For the Son of Man goes as it is written of him, but woe to that man by whom the Son of Man is betrayed!
>
> It would have been better for that man if he had not been born."

And as they were eating, he took bread, and after blessing it broke it and gave it to them, and said,

> "Take; this is my body."

And he took a cup, and when he had given thanks he gave it to them, and they all drank of it.

And he said to them,

> "This is my blood of the covenant, which is poured out for many.
>
> Truly, I say to you, I will not drink again of the fruit of the vine until that day when I drink it new in the kingdom of God."

LUKE 22:14-30

And when the hour came, he reclined at table, and the apostles with him. And he said to them,

> "I have earnestly desired to eat this Passover with you before I suffer.
>
> For I tell you I will not eat it until it is fulfilled in the kingdom of God."

And he took a cup, and when he had given thanks he said,

> "Take this, and divide it among yourselves.
>
> For I tell you that from now on I will not drink of the fruit of the vine until the kingdom of God comes."

And he took bread, and when he had given thanks, he broke it and gave it to them, saying,

"This is my body, which is given for you.

Do this in remembrance of me."

And likewise the cup after they had eaten, saying,

"This cup that is poured out for you is the new covenant in my blood.

But behold, the hand of him who betrays me is with me on the table.

For the Son of Man goes as it has been determined, but woe to that man by whom he is betrayed!"

And they began to question one another, which of them it could be who was going to do this.

A dispute also arose among them, as to which of them was to be regarded as the greatest. And he said to them,

"The kings of the Gentiles exercise lordship over them, and those in authority over them are called benefactors. But not so with you. Rather, let the greatest among you become as the youngest, and the leader as one who serves. For who is the greater, one who reclines at table or one who serves? Is it not the one who reclines at table? But I am among you as the one who serves.

"You are those who have stayed with me in my trials, and I assign to you, as my Father assigned to me, a kingdom, that you may eat and drink at my table in my kingdom and sit on thrones judging the twelve tribes of Israel."

COMMENTARY

On Thursday evening, Jesus and his disciples make their way to the room that has been prepared for this occasion and begin to eat the Passover meal. Each Gospel author includes different aspects of the arrangements and varying levels of detail concerning the events that took place and the words that were spoken during this

final meal.[5] The differences in arrangement do not represent contradictions but, as Matthew and Mark indicate, selective recount-
ings of some of the things that took place "as they were eating."[6]
This way of presenting the material does not necessarily require
chronological precision but rather indicates that the words were
spoken at some point during the meal. Likewise, the differences
in the degree of detail surrounding the words and actions of Jesus
and his followers are due to the evangelists' theological and literary selectivity in framing their presentation. No Gospel author
claims to record everything that was said or done that night. John
includes the greatest amount of detail with regard to Jesus's teaching and foot washing during the final meal and will therefore be
discussed separately below.

The Upper Room

Mark 14:15 and Luke 22:12 mention that the "upper room" was
large and furnished when Jesus and the disciples arrived. Most
peasant houses in Jerusalem were small, with two levels but only
one room. The presence of the large upper room indicates that the
owner was a person of means.

Typical eating arrangements would have three padded couches
arranged in an upside-down U-shape, with several participants per
couch. The food and drink would be available in the center on a
low table. They would recline on their left side, propped up on
their left elbow, with their feet pointing outward. Eating was done
with the right hand.

With this position visualized, one can understand John 13:23,
25, which describes John "reclining at table at Jesus's chest" (our
translation) and then "leaning back against Jesus." This most likely
means that John, the beloved disciple, was sitting in a place of honor
to the right of Jesus, who was likely in the middle of the center

---

[5] Obvious examples include how Luke mentions two cups (Luke 22:17–18, 20); how Jesus's
statement about his betrayer occurs after the meal in Luke and before the meal in Matthew and
Mark; and how John does not include information about the Lord's Supper but instead recounts
Jesus's washing of his disciples' feet.
[6] Matthew 26:21, 26; Mark 14:18, 22.

couch. The fact that Jesus gives the morsel of bread to Judas makes it likely that Judas was in the other place of honor, to Jesus's left. Since Peter motions to John to ask Jesus a question (John 13:24), it is likely that Peter is on one of the side couches opposite of John.

Seating Arrangements at the Last Supper

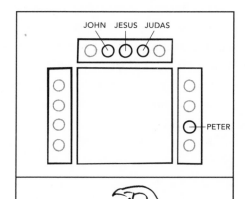

The Betrayer

As they are eating, Jesus makes a startling announcement: one of the Twelve, one of the men eating the Passover meal with him right then, is about to betray him.[7] This is shocking and upsetting news to the disciples, who instantly begin trying to identify the betrayer by questioning each other (Luke 22:23) and Jesus which one would betray their Master.[8] Jesus utters an ominous prophecy concerning his betrayer: "It would have been better for that man if he had not been born."[9] At that point, Judas does not foresee the end that will shortly fall upon him by his own hand, yet the announcement of doom must have sent shivers down his spine. Because each disciple

---

[7] Matthew 26:21–25; Mark 14:18–21; Luke 22:21–23.
[8] Matthew 26:22; Mark 14:19.
[9] Matthew 26:24; Mark 14:21; see also Luke 22:22.

is questioning Jesus, Judas likewise asks, "Is it I?" Jesus cryptically responds, "You have said so" (Matt. 26:25). The other disciples apparently did not pick up on this clue at the time, and John records that Judas left the dinner shortly thereafter (John 13:27–30).

The Lord's Supper

While they are eating, Jesus institutes the Lord's Supper. Luke includes some introductory words expressing Jesus's longing to eat this final Passover meal with his disciples and his realization that he would not eat it again until the coming of the kingdom of God (Luke 22:15–18). It was the "last supper" in a number of ways: the last meal that Jesus would eat with his disciples, the last meal that Jesus would eat in his pre-glorified body, and the final Passover meal of the old covenant. Jesus was likely looking forward to this meal so intensely because he knew that his upcoming death as the true Passover Lamb would bring a fulfillment to the long centuries of Passover celebrations that had pointed forward to the Messiah's final sacrifice for the sins of his people. The true meaning of the Passover sacrifice would soon be revealed and realized. Jesus knows that he will not engage in this kind of celebration with food and wine again until the final messianic banquet when God's people will experience eternal resurrection life in God's new creation.[10]

Jesus proceeds to utter the solemn words that are repeated each time his people celebrate the Lord's Supper: "Take, eat; this is my body. . . . Drink of it, all of you, for this is my blood of the covenant, which is poured out for many for the forgiveness of sins" (Matt. 26:26–28). "Do this in remembrance of me" (Luke 22:19). Paul's discussion of the Lord's Supper in 1 Corinthians 11:23–26 testifies to the centrality of this practice in the life of the early church. The apostle introduces an additional rationale for the practice when he argues that "as often as you eat this bread and drink the cup, you proclaim the Lord's death until he comes" (1 Cor. 11:26). In this way, the celebration of this ordinance looks back

---

[10] For further references to the final celebratory banquet at Christ's return see Isaiah 25:6–8; 65:13; Matthew 8:11; 22:1–14; 25:10; 26:29; Mark 14:25; Luke 13:29–30; 22:30; and Revelation 19:9.

in remembrance to Christ's finished work and looks forward with longing to his coming return. God's people have continued this practice to this very day.

Jesus himself explains the significance of the bread and wine.[11] The broken bread represents his body, which was about to be broken by blows, scourging, and crucifixion. The wine represents his blood, which is about to be poured out in order to inaugurate the new covenant and to bring forgiveness of sins to many. Just as the old covenant established by God with his people Israel at Sinai was inaugurated with the blood of sacrifices (Ex. 24:8), the new covenant, which would bring forgiveness of sins to all peoples, both Jews and Gentiles, was inaugurated by blood on a Roman cross. The language used by Jesus concerning his body being "given for you" and his blood being "poured out for many" points to the sacrificial nature of his death.[12]

Authority in Christ's Kingdom

Luke concludes his discussion of the Lord's Supper with material not found in Matthew and Mark (Luke 22:24–30). The disciples can sense that events are heading toward a climactic showdown, and they are convinced that they are on the right side, the side that will carry the day and result in status, power, and wealth. This preoccupation with a "human" assessment of power, achievement, and success leads, as it always will, to disputes and arguments concerning who is the greatest (Luke 22:24).[13] Jesus quickly puts an end to their discussion by making a powerful point: authority in Christ's kingdom is directly opposite that of Gentile rulers, and the greatest are the ones who serve.[14] Jesus assures his disciples that they will indeed reign with him someday (Luke 22:28–30),

---

[11] Matthew 26:26–28; Mark 14:22–24; Luke 22:19–20.

[12] Leviticus 17:11 makes clear that blood was tied to atonement in the Old Testament sacrificial system. This system, in its entirety as well as in its underlying premise that without the shedding of blood there is no forgiveness (Heb. 9:22), pointed ahead to Jesus as the ultimate substitutionary sacrifice for the sins of the world.

[13] The disciples had previously had similar arguments concerning which of them was the greatest (Matt. 20:20–28; Mark 9:33–34; Luke 9:46–48).

[14] These points were powerfully illustrated at that time by Jesus's washing of the disciples' feet (John 13:3–17), although Luke does not record this event.

but this day is not yet at hand—and as God's great narrative unfolds, it becomes increasingly clear that in the interim a great deal of persecution and suffering is yet to be experienced by both Jesus and his followers.

THE LAST SUPPER AND JESUS'S CLEANSING OF HIS COMMUNITY

During supper Jesus washes the disciples' feet, interacts with them, and delivers the Upper Room Discourse.

JOHN 13-14

Now before the Feast of the Passover, when Jesus knew that his hour had come to depart out of this world to the Father, having loved his own who were in the world, he loved them to the end.

During supper, when the devil had already put it into the heart of Judas Iscariot, Simon's son, to betray him, Jesus, knowing that the Father had given all things into his hands, and that he had come from God and was going back to God, rose from supper.

He laid aside his outer garments, and taking a towel, tied it around his waist. Then he poured water into a basin and began to wash the disciples' feet and to wipe them with the towel that was wrapped around him.

He came to Simon Peter, who said to him,

"Lord, do you wash my feet?"

Jesus answered him,

"What I am doing you do not understand now, but afterward you will understand."

Peter said to him,

"You shall never wash my feet."

Jesus answered him,

> "If I do not wash you, you have no share with me."

Simon Peter said to him,

> "Lord, not my feet only but also my hands and my head!"

Jesus said to him,

> "The one who has bathed does not need to wash, except for his feet, but is completely clean.
>
> And you are clean, but not every one of you."

For he knew who was to betray him; that was why he said, "Not all of you are clean."

When he had washed their feet and put on his outer garments and resumed his place, he said to them,

> "Do you understand what I have done to you? You call me Teacher and Lord, and you are right, for so I am. If I then, your Lord and Teacher, have washed your feet, you also ought to wash one another's feet. For I have given you an example, that you also should do just as I have done to you. Truly, truly, I say to you, a servant is not greater than his master, nor is a messenger greater than the one who sent him. If you know these things, blessed are you if you do them. I am not speaking of all of you; I know whom I have chosen. But the Scripture will be fulfilled,
>
> > 'He who ate my bread has lifted his heel against me.' [Ps. 41:9]
>
> I am telling you this now, before it takes place, that when it does take place you may believe that I am he. Truly, truly, I say to you, whoever receives the one I send receives me, and whoever receives me receives the one who sent me."

After saying these things, Jesus was troubled in his spirit, and testified,

> "Truly, truly, I say to you, one of you will betray me."

The disciples looked at one another, uncertain of whom he spoke.

One of his disciples, whom Jesus loved, was reclining at table at Jesus' side, so Simon Peter motioned to him to ask Jesus of whom he was speaking. So that disciple, leaning back against Jesus, said to him,

> "Lord, who is it?"

Jesus answered,

> "It is he to whom I will give this morsel of bread when I have dipped it."

So when he had dipped the morsel, he gave it to Judas, the son of Simon Iscariot. Then after he had taken the morsel, Satan entered into him. Jesus said to him,

> "What you are going to do, do quickly."

Now no one at the table knew why he said this to him. Some thought that, because Judas had the moneybag, Jesus was telling him, "Buy what we need for the feast," or that he should give something to the poor. So, after receiving the morsel of bread, he immediately went out. And it was night.

When he had gone out, Jesus said,

> "Now is the Son of Man glorified, and God is glorified in him. If God is glorified in him, God will also glorify him in himself, and glorify him at once. Little children, yet a little while I am with you. You will seek me, and just as I said to the Jews, so now I also say to you, 'Where I am going you cannot come.' A new commandment I give to you, that you love one another: just as I have loved you, you also are to love one another. By this all people will know that you are my disciples, if you have love for one another."

Simon Peter said to him,

> "Lord, where are you going?"

Jesus answered him,

"Where I am going you cannot follow me now, but you will follow afterward."

Peter said to him,

"Lord, why can I not follow you now?
I will lay down my life for you."

Jesus answered,

"Will you lay down your life for me?
Truly, truly, I say to you, the rooster will not crow till you have denied me three times.

"Let not your hearts be troubled. Believe in God; believe also in me. In my Father's house are many rooms. If it were not so, would I have told you that I go to prepare a place for you? And if I go and prepare a place for you, I will come again and will take you to myself, that where I am you may be also. And you know the way to where I am going."

Thomas said to him,

"Lord, we do not know where you are going. How can we know the way?"

Jesus said to him,

"I am the way, and the truth, and the life. No one comes to the Father except through me. If you had known me, you would have known my Father also. From now on you do know him and have seen him."

Philip said to him,

"Lord, show us the Father, and it is enough for us."

Jesus said to him,

"Have I been with you so long, and you still do not know me, Philip? Whoever has seen me has seen the Father. How can you say, 'Show us the Father'? Do you not believe that I am in the Father and the Father is in me? The words that I say to you I do not speak on my own authority, but the Father who dwells in me does his works. Believe me that I am in the Father and the Father is in me, or else believe on account of the works themselves.

"Truly, truly, I say to you, whoever believes in me will also do the works that I do; and greater works than these will he do, because I am going to the Father. Whatever you ask in my name, this I will do, that the Father may be glorified in the Son. If you ask me anything in my name, I will do it.

"If you love me, you will keep my commandments. And I will ask the Father, and he will give you another Helper, to be with you forever, even the Spirit of truth, whom the world cannot receive, because it neither sees him nor knows him. You know him, for he dwells with you and will be in you.

"I will not leave you as orphans; I will come to you. Yet a little while and the world will see me no more, but you will see me. Because I live, you also will live. In that day you will know that I am in my Father, and you in me, and I in you. Whoever has my commandments and keeps them, he it is who loves me. And he who loves me will be loved by my Father, and I will love him and manifest myself to him."

Judas (not Iscariot) said to him,

"Lord, how is it that you will manifest yourself to us, and not to the world?"

Jesus answered him,

"If anyone loves me, he will keep my word, and my Father will love him, and we will come to him and make our home with him. Whoever does not love me does not keep my words. And the word that you hear is not mine but the Father's who sent me.

"These things I have spoken to you while I am still with you. But the Helper, the Holy Spirit, whom the Father will send in my name, he will teach you all things and bring to your remembrance all that I have said to you. Peace I leave with you; my peace I give to you. Not as the world gives do I give to you. Let not your hearts be troubled, neither let them be afraid. You heard me say to you, 'I am going away, and I will come to you.' If you loved me, you would have rejoiced, because I am going to the Father, for the Father is greater than I. And now I have told you before it takes place, so that when it does take place you may believe. I will no longer talk much with you, for the ruler of this world is coming. He has no claim on me, but I do as the Father has commanded me, so that the world may know that I love the Father.

"Rise, let us go from here."

Jesus and the disciples sing a hymn together (probably from Psalms 113-118), then depart to the Mount of Olives.

MATTHEW 26:30

And when they had sung a hymn, they went out to the Mount of Olives.

MARK 14:26

And when they had sung a hymn, they went out to the Mount of Olives.

LUKE 22:39

And he came out and went, as was his custom, to the Mount of Olives, and the disciples followed him.

COMMENTARY

The setting in John parallels that of the Last Supper in Matthew, Mark, and Luke, but John focuses more on what Jesus taught his followers during and after the meal. Jesus, knowing that the end is near, spends his final hours instructing his twelve disciples, the representatives of his new messianic community.[15] John describes these final hours of intensive teaching and modeling of service by noting that Jesus "loved them [i.e., his followers] to the end" (John 13:1). Time is short, and every word and action matters. Jesus has a clear understanding of the suffering and difficulty that lie ahead, but the disciples are still unaware of the rapid succession of events that are about to happen and are unprepared for Jesus's departure and their future life without his physical presence. This final discourse covers a lot of ground, but several themes recur, including Jesus's continuing mission through the Spirit and his disciples, and the centrality of love, joy, and peace in the lives of Jesus's followers.[16]

The Literal Cleansing: Jesus Washes His Disciples' Feet (John 13:1-17)

Jesus and the disciples find themselves in the middle of an embarrassing situation: there is apparently no servant to wash the feet of the guests (as would have been culturally appropriate and expected), and the disciples have neglected to do so or are too proud to engage in such a menial task. Thus, they have reclined to eat the Last Supper with dirty feet, filthy from traveling on Jerusalem's dusty roads. Jesus perceives this situation as an opportunity to communicate two valuable lessons.

First, believers are "clean" (i.e., converted and regenerated) but still need continual spiritual cleansing (i.e., confession and forgiveness). Jesus makes this point in response to Peter's misunderstanding of the situation (John 13:6–11). Peter and the other ten disciples were "clean" (though not yet regenerated) and only needed partial "cleansing," in contrast to Judas, who was not "clean" and for whom temporary partial "cleansing" was not

---

[15] John emphasizes that Jesus knew the hour had come to depart from the world and return to his Father (John 13:1, 3; 16:28; 17:11). John 13:1, 3 makes clear that Jesus viewed the temporary nature of his upcoming suffering from an eternal perspective—he was departing from the world and going back to God (see also Heb. 12:2).

[16] These themes occur as follows: mission (John 14:15–27; 15:26–16:15; 17:18); love (John 13:1, 34–35; 15:9–13; 17:26); joy (John 15:11; 16:22–24; 17:13); and peace (John 14:27; 16:33).

enough. Believers do not need to be "resaved" every day yet are in need of daily spiritual cleansing and renewal by the Holy Spirit.

Second, Jesus's example of washing his disciples' feet teaches us the need for loving, self-sacrificial service to each other (John 13:12–17): "For I have given you an example, that you also should do just as I have done to you" (John 13:15).[17] The foot-washing episode foreshadows the crucifixion by displaying Jesus's attitude of self-sacrifice, love, and service—attitudes that must characterize Jesus's followers (see Phil. 2:1–8). As an anticipatory commentary on the cross, the foot washing illumines the underlying motivation for the cross: God's sacrificial love for the people he has made (see John 3:16).

The Figurative Cleansing: The Betrayer Departs (John 13:18-30)

Jesus had drawn attention to one who was not clean, a betrayer, earlier in the foot-washing episode (John 13:10–11), but he now proceeds to devote all his attention to the subject because he is "troubled in his spirit" (John 13:21). Jesus's foreknowledge of Judas's betrayal in fulfillment of Scripture highlights God's sovereignty and control over all that was about to take place.[18] Although, at the time, the betrayal must have seemed to the eleven disciples like a nightmare spinning out of control, everything was completely under God's providential care and in keeping with his sovereign plan (see Acts 2:23; 4:27–28).

Even though John, at Peter's prompting, asks Jesus directly concerning the identity of the betrayer, the disciples remain uncertain as to which one of them Jesus has in mind. Judas has apparently concealed his motives and intentions quite well—not even his closest friends know what is in his heart. John draws attention to the satanic inspiration of Judas's betrayal (John 13:2, 27).[19] This realization does not remove Judas's guilt or responsibility in

---

[17] The practice of foot washing should be recast in most modern cultures where people do not wear sandals and walk everywhere they go. It symbolizes any humble act of service (see 1 Tim. 5:10).

[18] Jesus's foreknowledge is evident in John 6:70–71; 13:2, 10–11, 19; in John 13:8 he cites Psalm 41:9 as being fulfilled.

[19] See also Luke 22:3.

the matter but highlights the spiritual warfare that was playing itself out through human actors and would soon culminate in Satan's apparent victory followed by God's ultimate triumph (see Gen. 3:15). The darkness of Judas's soul is subtly highlighted when John ominously notes that Judas went out when "it was night" (John 13:30).

Jesus's new messianic community has now been cleansed both literally (the foot washing) and figuratively (the removal of the betrayer) and has thus been prepared for his final instructions.

THE FAREWELL DISCOURSE BEGINS (JOHN 13:31-14:31)

At the beginning of the Farewell Discourse, Jesus highlights what is to be the defining characteristic of his followers: love for one another (John 13:34–35). This love is to be so clear and visible that by observing it, outsiders will know that Jesus's disciples are his followers. Sadly, many unbelievers today would probably not mention love as the primary characteristic of Christians.

From this point forward, the Farewell Discourse progresses as Jesus responds to a series of misunderstandings and questions by his disciples. First, Peter asks Jesus where he is going and why he cannot follow Jesus now (John 13:36–37). Jesus responds by noting that his disciples will indeed follow him to the place where he is going, but not right then (John 13:36), and that he is going to prepare a place for them (John 14:1–4).[20] In light of this future reunion, the disciples are to put aside fear and uncertainty and place their faith in God (John 14:1).

Thomas then takes the place of Peter as the questioner and asks how the disciples are going to follow Jesus since they do not know the way (John 14:5). Jesus responds with the justly famous words, "I am the way, and the truth, and the life. No one comes to the Father except through me" (John 14:6). Thomas was thinking of a literal, earthly destination that could be accessed by human

---

[20] Jesus also takes this opportunity to predict Peter's denials in response to Peter's claim that he would lay down his life for Jesus (John 13:37–38). Jesus is the one who would lay down his life for his followers, not the other way around.

travel, while Jesus was speaking of an eternal destiny that could be reached only by allegiance to himself.

Philip makes the next statement: "Lord, show us the Father, and it is enough for us" (John 14:8). In a subtle way, this request, too, reveals unbelief, or at least lack of understanding. Jesus responds by emphasizing his unity with the Father: "Whoever has seen me has seen the Father" (John 14:9). Jesus also includes the Holy Spirit in his response by promising another "Helper," the "Spirit of truth," who will be with his followers forever (John 14:16–17). Whoever believes in Jesus will perform greater works (John 14:12), and whoever loves Jesus must demonstrate this love through obedience to his commandments (John 14:21).

Judas (not Iscariot) asks the final question in this section: "Lord, how is it that you will manifest yourself to us, and not to the world?" (John 14:22). This seems to be a reasonable query. If you and I had been among the disciples in the upper room, one of us would likely have asked Jesus the very same question. Why would Jesus appear only to his followers and not to unbelievers as well? Would that not be a great way to manifest himself to those who didn't already believe in him? Jesus initially responds by emphasizing that those who love and obey him will be set apart from the world by being indwelt by the Father, himself, and the Holy Spirit (John 14:23–26). What is more, while the revelation is only for the disciples, they will be sent to the whole world (John 17:18; 20:21). In addition, it is also likely that John 15:1–16:4 expands upon this answer to Judas's question.

Finally, in light of the fact that there is not much time left, Jesus exhorts his followers to maintain peace in light of his coming departure—a departure that is causing his followers a great deal of confusion and turmoil (John 14:27–31). This first part of the Farewell Discourse ends with Jesus instructing his disciples to get up and depart with him, presumably to move on to the garden of Gethsemane (John 14:31).[21]

---

[21] Because the discourse continues in chapter 15 without any indication of actual geographical movement, some interpreters think that this reference to a departure indicates a literary seam— that is, a later editor combined two originally separate literary units (John 13–14 and John

At this, Jesus and the disciples sing a hymn together and then depart toward the Mount of Olives. Jews traditionally sang Psalms 113–118 during the Passover celebration, culminating in Psalm 118, so it is very likely that this was the final hymn sung by Jesus and his disciples before leaving the upper room and walking to the garden of Gethsemane. The highly significant words of Psalm 118:22–23 were likely ringing in Jesus's ears as he contemplated the horrors ahead of him: "The stone that the builders rejected has become the cornerstone. This is the LORD's doing; it is marvelous in our eyes." Jesus had previously quoted this verse when interpreting the parable of the vineyard—he was the heir whom the vineyard's tenants had rejected and killed.[22] The early Christians, likewise, interpreted the verse with reference to Jesus: he is the cornerstone, the only way to salvation (Acts 4:10–12), and the foundation of God's spiritual house made up of his people.[23] The words of this final hymn surely brought comfort to Jesus by reminding him that his coming rejection and suffering were the very means by which God would make him the cornerstone of salvation for all who believe. With this reassurance, he would be better equipped to weather the dark night ahead.

THE FAREWELL DISCOURSE CONTINUES

Jesus continues to teach his disciples and prays to God.

JOHN 15-17

"I am the true vine, and my Father is the vinedresser. Every branch in me that does not bear fruit he takes away, and every branch that does bear fruit he prunes, that it may bear more fruit. Already you

15–17) into one discourse (John 13–17). However, it is more likely that Jesus and his followers left the upper room at John 14:31 and that the interchanges in John 15–16 occurred on the way to the garden of Gethsemane, perhaps while Jesus and his disciples were walking past vineyards along the way, which would have provided a fitting backdrop for Jesus's instruction. Another possibility is that Jesus's "vine" metaphor was occasioned by the golden vine overhanging the main entrance to the temple.
[22] Matthew 21:42; Mark 12:10, 11; Luke 20:17.
[23] Ephesians 2:19–20; 1 Peter 2:4–7; see also Isaiah 28:16.

are clean because of the word that I have spoken to you. Abide in me, and I in you. As the branch cannot bear fruit by itself, unless it abides in the vine, neither can you, unless you abide in me. I am the vine; you are the branches. Whoever abides in me and I in him, he it is that bears much fruit, for apart from me you can do nothing. If anyone does not abide in me he is thrown away like a branch and withers; and the branches are gathered, thrown into the fire, and burned. If you abide in me, and my words abide in you, ask whatever you wish, and it will be done for you. By this my Father is glorified, that you bear much fruit and so prove to be my disciples. As the Father has loved me, so have I loved you. Abide in my love. If you keep my commandments, you will abide in my love, just as I have kept my Father's commandments and abide in his love. These things I have spoken to you, that my joy may be in you, and that your joy may be full.

"This is my commandment, that you love one another as I have loved you. Greater love has no one than this, that someone lay down his life for his friends. You are my friends if you do what I command you. No longer do I call you servants, for the servant does not know what his master is doing; but I have called you friends, for all that I have heard from my Father I have made known to you. You did not choose me, but I chose you and appointed you that you should go and bear fruit and that your fruit should abide, so that whatever you ask the Father in my name, he may give it to you. These things I command you, so that you will love one another.

"If the world hates you, know that it has hated me before it hated you. If you were of the world, the world would love you as its own; but because you are not of the world, but I chose you out of the world, therefore the world hates you. Remember the word that I said to you:

'A servant is not greater than his master.'

If they persecuted me, they will also persecute you. If they kept my word, they will also keep yours. But all these things they will do to you on account of my name, because they do not know him who sent me. If I had not come and spoken to them, they would not have been guilty of sin, but now they have no excuse for their sin. Whoever hates me hates my Father also. If I had not done among them the works that no one else did, they would not be guilty of sin, but now they have seen and hated both me and my Father. But the word that is written in their Law must be fulfilled:

'They hated me without a cause.' [Ps. 69:4]

"But when the Helper comes, whom I will send to you from the Father, the Spirit of truth, who proceeds from the Father, he will bear witness about me. And you also will bear witness, because you have been with me from the beginning.

"I have said all these things to you to keep you from falling away. They will put you out of the synagogues. Indeed, the hour is coming when whoever kills you will think he is offering service to God. And they will do these things because they have not known the Father, nor me. But I have said these things to you, that when their hour comes you may remember that I told them to you.

"I did not say these things to you from the beginning, because I was with you. But now I am going to him who sent me, and none of you asks me,

'Where are you going?'

But because I have said these things to you, sorrow has filled your heart. Nevertheless, I tell you the truth: it is to your advantage that I go away, for if I do not go away, the Helper will not come to you. But if I go, I will send him to you. And when he comes, he will convict the world concerning sin and righteousness and judgment: concerning sin, because they do not believe in me; concerning righteousness, because I go to the Father, and you will see me no longer; concerning judgment, because the ruler of this world is judged.

"I still have many things to say to you, but you cannot bear them now. When the Spirit of truth comes, he will guide you into all the truth, for he will not speak on his own authority, but whatever he hears he will speak, and he will declare to you the things that are to come. He will glorify me, for he will take what is mine and declare it to you. All that the Father has is mine; therefore I said that he will take what is mine and declare it to you.

"A little while, and you will see me no longer; and again a little while, and you will see me."

So some of his disciples said to one another,

"What is this that he says to us,

'A little while, and you will not see me, and again a little while, and you will see me';

and,

'because I am going to the Father'?"

So they were saying,

"What does he mean by 'a little while'? We do not know what he is talking about."

Jesus knew that they wanted to ask him, so he said to them,

"Is this what you are asking yourselves, what I meant by saying,

'A little while and you will not see me, and again a little while and you will see me'?

Truly, truly, I say to you, you will weep and lament, but the world will rejoice. You will be sorrowful, but your sorrow will turn into joy. When a woman is giving birth, she has sorrow because her hour has come, but when she has delivered the baby, she no longer remembers the anguish, for joy that a human being has been born into the world. So also you have sorrow now, but I will see you again, and your hearts will rejoice, and no one will take your joy from you. In that day you will ask nothing of me. Truly, truly, I say to you, whatever you ask of the Father in my name, he will give it to you. Until now you have asked nothing in my name. Ask, and you will receive, that your joy may be full.

"I have said these things to you in figures of speech. The hour is coming when I will no longer speak to you in figures of speech but will tell you plainly about the Father. In that day you will ask in my name, and I do not say to you that I will ask the Father on your behalf; for the Father himself loves you, because you have loved me and have believed that I came from God. I came from the Father and have come into the world, and now I am leaving the world and going to the Father."

His disciples said,

"Ah, now you are speaking plainly and not using figurative speech! Now we know that you know all things and do not need anyone to question you; this is why we believe that you came from God."

Jesus answered them,

"Do you now believe? Behold, the hour is coming, indeed it has come, when you will be scattered, each to his own home, and will leave me alone. Yet I am not alone, for the Father is with me. I have said these things to you, that in me you may have peace. In the world you will have tribulation. But take heart; I have overcome the world."

When Jesus had spoken these words, he lifted up his eyes to heaven, and said,

"Father, the hour has come; glorify your Son that the Son may glorify you, since you have given him authority over all flesh, to give eternal life to all whom you have given him. And this is eternal life, that they know you the only true God, and Jesus Christ whom you have sent. I glorified you on earth, having accomplished the work that you gave me to do. And now, Father, glorify me in your own presence with the glory that I had with you before the world existed.

"I have manifested your name to the people whom you gave me out of the world. Yours they were, and you gave them to me, and they have kept your word. Now they know that everything that you have given me is from you. For I have given them the words that you gave me, and they have received them and have come to know in truth that I came from you; and they have believed that you sent me. I am praying for them. I am not praying for the world but for those whom you have given me, for they are yours. All mine are yours, and yours are mine, and I am glorified in them. And I am no longer in the world, but they are in the world, and I am coming to you. Holy Father, keep them in your name, which you have given me, that they may be one, even as we are one. While I was with them, I kept them in your name, which you have given me. I have guarded them, and not one of them has been lost except the son of destruction, that the Scripture might be fulfilled. But now I am coming to you, and these things I speak in the world, that they may have my joy fulfilled in themselves. I have given them your word, and the world has hated them because they are not of the world, just as I am not of the world. I do not ask that you take them out of the world, but that you keep them from the evil one. They are not of the world, just as I am not of the world. Sanctify them in the truth; your word is truth. As you sent me into the world, so I have sent them into the world. And for their sake I consecrate myself, that they also may be sanctified in truth.

"I do not ask for these only, but also for those who will believe in me through their word, that they may all be one, just as you, Father, are in me, and I in you, that they also may be in us, so that the world may believe that you have sent me. The glory that you have given me I have given to them, that they may be one even as we are one, I in them and you in me, that they may become perfectly one, so that the world may know that you sent me and loved them even as you loved me. Father, I desire that they also, whom you have given me, may be with me where I am, to see my glory that you have given me because you loved me before the foundation of the world. O righteous Father, even though the world does not know you, I know you, and these know that you have sent me. I made known to them your name, and I will continue to make it known, that the love with which you have loved me may be in them, and I in them."

COMMENTARY

The Vine and the Branches (John 15:1-17)

Jesus continues his answer to Judas's question[24] by using the illustration of a vine and its branches.[25] The Old Testament often used the image of a vineyard or vine to represent Israel, particularly with regard to their failure to produce fruit and the resulting judgment. Here Jesus presents himself as the true vine, the true Israel, who will fulfill Israel's destiny and enable his disciples—the "branches"—to bear fruit by remaining in him. By virtue of their union with him, Jesus's followers are thus part of the new fruit-bearing Israel.[26]

In the illustration, God, the vinedresser, does two things to maximize the fruit production of the branches (Jesus's followers). First, he prunes them so they can be more fruitful (John 15:2). This pruning involves cutting away anything—interests, activities, habits—that hinder growth and effectiveness (fruit bearing). Historically, this was seen in the original disciples, who grew in spiritual maturity and became more effective in their mission for God. Second, the vinedresser removes and burns fruitless branches (John 15:2, 6). This was the case with Judas Iscariot, who was removed from among Jesus's followers and became the object of God's judgment.

---

[24] Remember that this is the other disciple named Judas; the betrayer has already left the disciples to carry out his satanic plan.

[25] Judas had asked, "Lord, how is it that you will manifest yourself to us, and not to the world?" (John 14:22).

[26] Note that the notion of Jesus as true Israel and the church as new Israel does not necessarily mean there is no future hope/plan for ethnic Israel (what theologians call "supercessionism").

Today and every day until Jesus's return, true followers of Jesus abide in him and bear much fruit by continuing in a daily, personal relationship with their Lord and Master. This relationship is characterized and nurtured by adhering to Jesus's words (John 15:7) and by obeying his commandments, particularly the command to love one another (John 15:10–14; see also 13:34–35). Those who remain in Christ have confidence in prayer and know that God will hear and answer their requests because they desire what Christ desires and pray accordingly, in keeping with his will (John 15:7).

Finally, one (if not the) primary point of the vine and branch illustration is the believer's complete dependence on Jesus: apart from remaining in a daily relationship with him, his followers can do nothing of eternal value (John 15:4–5). Not that it is impossible for anyone to do anything good on their own, but anything of true, lasting significance must be done by God through us. Believers will never outgrow their daily need to abide in Christ. Jesus has now answered the first part of Judas's question (John 14:22) by explaining that his followers are set apart from the world by being connected to the vine. Jesus will manifest himself to his followers through the Holy Spirit because they remain in him.

The World's Hatred of Jesus's Followers (John 15:18–16:4a)

Jesus then proceeds to answer the second part of Judas's question (John 14:22) by describing why he will not manifest himself to the world. In contrast to believers who continue in a unique love relationship with Jesus, the world hates the Father as well as Jesus and his followers. Jesus reassures his disciples that the world hated him first but makes clear that the world will hate them also because they are no longer, spiritually speaking, part of the world (John 15:18–19).

The world's hatred and persecution only serve to exacerbate its guilt, particularly because Jesus's divine works were met with increasing hatred (John 15:21–25). The future judgment of sinful humanity would not come because they had no opportunity to repent—to the contrary, they had seen Jesus's signs and heard his teaching—but because they had ample opportunity for repentance and still refused to believe (see also John 12:37–40).

The world's hatred will be expressed in concrete acts of persecution (John 15:20). In the future, Jesus says, his followers will be put out of the synagogues and even be killed for their faith (John 16:2). Part of the purpose of Jesus's advance warning was to prepare his followers in order to keep them from falling away in the midst of persecution (John 16:1). Once the world had killed him, it would target his followers. Jesus informs his disciples that the Holy Spirit will continue to bear witness in the midst of the hateful world and urges them to bear faithful witness, thus continuing Jesus's mission on this earth even after he is no longer physically present with them (John 15:26–27).

The Advantages of Jesus's Departure (John 16:4b-15)

As the disciples slowly begin to realize that Jesus's departure is imminent (though they are still not completely clear on all the details), Jesus proactively speaks to them in order to alleviate their sorrow, fear, and uncertainty. Counterintuitively, Jesus argues that it will in fact be better for him to leave so that he can send the Holy Spirit, who will convict the world of its sin, lack of righteousness, and coming judgment and will guide the disciples in all truth. In the future, the Holy Spirit will act as the bridge between Jesus and his disciples by taking what belongs to Jesus and declaring it to the disciples (John 16:13–15). The physical removal of Jesus from the earth will inaugurate the age of the Spirit, the next stage of salvation history.

The "Little While" (John 16:16-33)

Jesus proceeds to make a statement that causes a great deal of consternation and discussion among his disciples: "A little while, and you will see me no longer; and again a little while, and you will see me" (John 16:16). What does Jesus mean by a "little while" (John 16:17–19)? Jesus clears up the confusion by means of an analogy from human birth in which a time of great pain and sorrow is followed by great joy (John 16:21–22); the pain and the wait are almost inconsequential in comparison with the joyful blessing that results (see 2 Cor. 4:17).

Since this discourse took place on Thursday night and Jesus would be crucified Friday afternoon, the first "little while" spanned less than twenty-four hours. The crucifixion would lead to a period of pain and suffering—the next "little while"—which would last until Jesus's resurrection and appearances when sorrow and pain would be replaced with an overwhelming joy that could not be taken away (John 16:22). Subsequent to the resurrection, the disciples of Jesus must pray with confidence to the Father in Jesus's name, knowing that God will hear their prayers and answer them (John 16:23–24).

Jesus further notes that at that future time—his post-resurrection appearances—he will no longer speak in figures of speech as he is presently doing (John 16:25). The disciples find this to be great news and, as usual, assume that they understand more than they actually do (John 16:29–31). Their awareness and understanding of the significance of the coming events is still largely lacking, and not until after Jesus's resurrection from the dead will they truly understand the meaning of his words.

Jesus closes the Farewell Discourse and transitions to what is sometimes called his "High Priestly Prayer" (John 17) by noting that, despite his disciples' claims to believe in his divine origin, they all will soon be scattered and abandon him (John 16:32). Despite this ominous prediction, Jesus concludes with words of comfort: "I have said these things to you, that in me you may have peace. In the world you will have tribulation. But take heart; I have overcome the world" (John 16:33).

Jesus Prays for Himself (John 17:1–5)

John concludes his presentation of the Farewell Discourse by recounting the longest recorded prayer of Jesus in the entire New Testament. Jesus's prayer here, immediately prior to his arrest, trial,

The High Priestly Prayer

The Father Gave the Son . . .	John 17
authority to give eternal life	v. 2
people out of this world	vv. 2, 6, 9, 24
work to accomplish	v. 4
words	v. 8
his name	vv. 11, 12
glory	vv. 22, 24

The Son Gives Believers . . .	John 17
eternal life	v. 2
the Father's word	vv. 8, 14
manifestation of the Father's name	vv. 6, 26
glory	v. 22

The Son Asks the Father to . . .	John 17
glorify him	vv. 1, 5
keep believers in the Father's name	v. 11
keep believers from the Evil One	v. 15
sanctify believers in the truth	v. 17
make believers one	v. 21

Jesus's Followers and the World	John 17
they are sent into the world	v. 18
they are in the world	v. 11
they are not of the world	v. 16
the world has hated them	v. 14
their unity with each other and union with God may cause the world to believe the Father sent the Son	v. 21

and crucifixion, fits his earlier habit of praying for extended periods of time before important decisions and events.[27] Jesus's prayer neatly divides into three sections: his prayer for himself, his prayer for his disciples, and his prayer for future believers.

Jesus's prayer for himself centers on glory. He prays that God will glorify the Son so that the Son might glorify the Father (John 17:1). Jesus had glorified God on earth by accomplishing his mission and now longs for the glory that he shared with God before the world began (John 17:4–5). In these first verses of the prayer, Jesus stands out as an example for believers to follow. His life has been entirely devoted to the pursuit of God's glory by accomplishing the work God had given him to do. This single-minded devotion and passion for God's glory ought to characterize every true disciple. Finally, Jesus's definition of eternal life in John 17:3 is quite significant. Eternal life is not wholly reserved for some future time but actually begins in the present as people come to know and believe in God through Jesus.

---

[27] See, for example, his prayer before appointing the twelve disciples (Luke 6:12) and his prayer in the garden of Gethsemane recorded in Matthew, Mark, and Luke.

Jesus Prays for His Disciples (John 17:6-19)

Most of Jesus's prayer for his disciples is commentary surrounding three central requests.[28] First, Jesus requests that God "keep them in your name . . . that they may be one, even as we are one" (John 17:11). Jesus's greatest prayer is that God will keep his disciples from falling away and preserve them in unity—a unity reflecting the very unity that the Son shares with the Father. Unity should never be attained at the cost of truth, yet unity is essential among God's people, particularly in regard to a shared mind and purpose and mutual love in the work of fulfilling Christ's mission to the world.

Second, Jesus prays not that God will take his disciples out of the world but that God would "keep them from the evil one" (John 17:15). If Jesus were to take his followers out of the world, there would be no one to carry on his mission to the world throughout the remainder of human history! As with his first request, Jesus here asks God to keep and preserve his followers from the Evil One and from evil in general.

Finally, Jesus asks God to "sanctify them in the truth; your word is truth" (John 17:17). Sanctification is a lifelong process whereby believers progressively grow in holiness and purity in their thoughts, words, and actions. From Jesus's prayer, we can draw confidence that God is proactively involved in sanctifying us and that God's Word will play an important part in that process. The sanctification of believers enables us to engage in effective witness to a hostile world, thereby continuing Jesus's mission until his return.

Jesus Prays for Future Believers (John 17:20-26)

Jesus anticipates that his mission will indeed be effectively continued by his disciples and prays accordingly for those who will believe in the future based upon their witness. Jesus's primary request for these future believers is unity, modeled after the unity of the Son and Father. Jesus makes clear that unity among his followers will be one of the key components of fulfilling his mission and bring-

---

[28] The three requests are found in John 17:11, 15, and 17.

ing the world from hostility and hatred to faith (John 17:21–23).[29] Following the completion of this prayer, John recounts the arrival of Jesus and his disciples at the garden of Gethsemane (John 18:1).

———•◦•———

JESUS PREDICTS PETER'S DENIALS

Jesus foretells Peter's denials.

MATTHEW 26:31-35

Then Jesus said to them,

> "You will all fall away because of me this night. For it is written,
>
>> 'I will strike the shepherd, and the sheep of the flock will be scattered.' [Zech. 13:7]
>
> But after I am raised up, I will go before you to Galilee."

Peter answered him,

> "Though they all fall away because of you, I will never fall away."

Jesus said to him,

> "Truly, I tell you, this very night, before the rooster crows, you will deny me three times."

Peter said to him,

> "Even if I must die with you, I will not deny you!"

And all the disciples said the same.

MARK 14:27-31

And Jesus said to them,

> "You will all fall away, for it is written,
>
>> 'I will strike the shepherd, and the sheep will be scattered.' [Zech. 13:7]

---

[29] This is parallel to the function of love among believers in John 13:34–35.

But after I am raised up, I will go before you to Galilee."

Peter said to him,

"Even though they all fall away, I will not."

And Jesus said to him,

"Truly, I tell you, this very night, before the rooster crows twice, you will deny me three times."

But he said emphatically,

"If I must die with you, I will not deny you."

And they all said the same.

LUKE 22:31-34

[Jesus said:]

"Simon, Simon, behold, Satan demanded to have you, that he might sift you like wheat, but I have prayed for you that your faith may not fail.

And when you have turned again, strengthen your brothers."

Peter said to him,

"Lord, I am ready to go with you both to prison and to death."

Jesus said,

"I tell you, Peter, the rooster will not crow this day, until you deny three times that you know me."

COMMENTARY

After earlier shocking his disciples with the announcement that a betrayer is in their midst, Jesus again shakes them up with the prediction that they will all fall away from him that very night.[30]

---

[30] Matthew 26:31 and Mark 14:27 place this event after leaving the upper room, while Luke and John place the prediction in the Upper Room Discourse. It is quite possible that such an alarming and startling prediction resulted in multiple discussions. This hypothesis is strengthened by the different details included in Luke and John. Matthew and Mark indicate that Peter repeatedly

According to Matthew and Mark, Jesus bases this prediction on the prophecy contained in Zechariah 13:7 but assures his disciples that after he is raised up he will go before them to Galilee.[31] This prediction that they will fall away does not indicate that the eleven will cease to be Jesus's disciples but that they will fail in the face of persecution that night. Jesus promises restoration even as he predicts failure.

Peter famously contradicts Jesus's prediction by claiming that he will never fall away and will follow Jesus to prison and death.[32] Peter persists in his well-meaning but ultimately arrogant claims in spite of Jesus's bluntly telling him that he will deny Jesus three times before the rooster crows.[33] The other disciples, influenced by Peter's shortsighted show of confidence, make similar claims.[34]

Luke includes some additional details in his report of this incident. Satan has desired to defeat the disciples (the "you" in Luke 22:31 is plural), but Jesus has prayed for Peter (the "you" in Luke 22:32 is singular), that his faith will not fail and that after repenting he will strengthen the other disciples. This prayer that Peter's faith will not fail fits remarkably well with the content of Jesus's prayer for his disciples in John 17:6–19. The mention of Satan's activity that fateful night matches his involvement in Judas's betrayal.[35] Satan did not just want to kill Jesus through the betrayal; he intended to destroy the faith of all of Jesus's followers. Jesus is confident that his prayer will counteract and defeat Satan's intentions.

---

refused to acknowledge Jesus's prediction and the rest of the disciples said the same—a situation possibly resulting in a repetition of the conversation.

[31] Jesus possibly made this reference to Galilee to defuse expectations of an immediate revolution in Jerusalem.

[32] Matthew 26:33, 35; Mark 14:29, 31; Luke 22:33; John 13:37.

[33] The reference to the rooster crowing was an idiomatic way of describing the coming of dawn, and since roosters regularly crow multiple times, often minutes apart, Mark's reference to the rooster crowing twice points to the same general time period: Peter will deny Christ before sunrise.

[34] Matthew 26:35; Mark 14:31.

[35] Luke 22:3; John 13:2, 27; see also Job 1–2 for a similar request from Satan.

JESUS ISSUES FINAL PRACTICAL COMMANDS

Jesus gives his eleven disciples practical commands about supplies and provisions.

LUKE 22:35-38

And he said to them,

> "When I sent you out with no moneybag or knapsack or sandals, did you lack anything?"

They said,

> "Nothing."

He said to them,

> "But now let the one who has a moneybag take it, and likewise a knapsack.

And let the one who has no sword sell his cloak and buy one.

For I tell you that this Scripture must be fulfilled in me:

> 'And he was numbered with the transgressors.' [Isa. 53:12]

For what is written about me has its fulfillment."

And they said,

> "Look, Lord, here are two swords."

And he said to them,

> "It is enough."

COMMENTARY

Luke includes some final practical instructions by Jesus not contained in any of the other Gospel accounts. In contrast to Jesus's earlier instructions to his disciples that they should go out on their mission with no moneybag, knapsack, or sandals, Jesus now instructs them to go on their mission, after his departure, fully prepared for whatever might come (Luke 22:35–37).

Jesus's reference to the possession of a sword can be interpreted in two ways. First, some argue that Jesus's command to buy a sword is metaphorical and points to the need to be ready for spiritual warfare (compare Paul's words in Eph. 6:10–17). This interpretation is supported by the fact that Jesus will shortly prohibit the use of swords in his defense.[36] In this view, the disciples misinterpret Jesus when they produce two swords, and Jesus rebukes them when he tersely says, "It is enough" (Luke 22:38).

Second, perhaps less likely, Jesus may have meant that his disciples should travel with literal swords for self-defense and protection. The fact that the disciples had two swords in their possession may indicate that Jesus had not previously prevented them from carrying weapons (unless, of course, they did so in an unauthorized manner in the present instance).

From the Upper Room to the Garden of Gethsemane

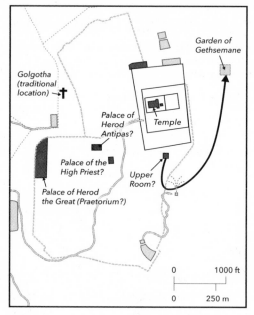

---

[36] Matthew 26:51–52; Luke 22:49–51; John 18:10–11.

THE GARDEN OF GETHSEMANE

Jesus and the disciples go to Gethsemane, where he struggles in prayer and they struggle to stay awake late into the night.

MATTHEW 26:36-46

Then Jesus went with them to a place called Gethsemane, and he said to his disciples,

> "Sit here, while I go over there and pray."

And taking with him Peter and the two sons of Zebedee, he began to be sorrowful and troubled. Then he said to them,

> "My soul is very sorrowful, even to death;
> remain here, and watch with me."

And going a little farther he fell on his face and prayed, saying,

> "My Father, if it be possible, let this cup pass from me;
> nevertheless, not as I will, but as you will."

And he came to the disciples and found them sleeping.

And he said to Peter,

> "So, could you not watch with me one hour?
> Watch and pray that you may not enter into temptation.
> The spirit indeed is willing, but the flesh is weak."

Again, for the second time, he went away and prayed,

> "My Father, if this cannot pass unless I drink it, your will be done."

And again he came and found them sleeping, for their eyes were heavy.

So, leaving them again, he went away and prayed for the third time, saying the same words again.

Then he came to the disciples and said to them,

> "Sleep and take your rest later on.

See, the hour is at hand, and the Son of Man is betrayed into the hands of sinners.

Rise, let us be going; see, my betrayer is at hand."

MARK 14:32-42

And they went to a place called Gethsemane.

And he said to his disciples,

"Sit here while I pray."

And he took with him Peter and James and John, and began to be greatly distressed and troubled. And he said to them,

"My soul is very sorrowful, even to death.
Remain here and watch."

And going a little farther, he fell on the ground and prayed that, if it were possible, the hour might pass from him.

And he said,

"Abba, Father, all things are possible for you.
Remove this cup from me.
Yet not what I will, but what you will."

And he came and found them sleeping, and he said to Peter,

"Simon, are you asleep?
Could you not watch one hour?
Watch and pray that you may not enter into temptation.
The spirit indeed is willing, but the flesh is weak."

And again he went away and prayed, saying the same words.

And again he came and found them sleeping, for their eyes were very heavy, and they did not know what to answer him.

And he came the third time and said to them,

"Are you still sleeping and taking your rest? It is enough; the hour has come. The Son of Man is betrayed into the hands of sinners. Rise, let us be going; see, my betrayer is at hand."

LUKE 22:40-46

And when he came to the place, he said to them,

> "Pray that you may not enter into temptation."

And he withdrew from them about a stone's throw, and knelt down and prayed, saying,

> "Father, if you are willing, remove this cup from me.
> Nevertheless, not my will, but yours, be done."

[[And there appeared to him an angel from heaven, strengthening him.

And being in an agony he prayed more earnestly; and his sweat became like great drops of blood falling down to the ground.]][37]

And when he rose from prayer, he came to the disciples and found them sleeping for sorrow, and he said to them,

> "Why are you sleeping?
> Rise and pray that you may not enter into temptation."

COMMENTARY

Gethsemane

Since Deuteronomy 16:1–7 indicates that the Passover evening had to be spent in Jerusalem (including the Mount of Olives), Jesus and his eleven remaining disciples do not return to Bethany as they had done throughout the week. Instead, after leaving the upper room and their Passover meal, they cross down into the Kidron Valley to the east of the city walls and ascend back up to the garden of Gethsemane, a place the disciples evidently knew well and where they had often spent time with Jesus (John 18:2). Gethsemane, derived from a word meaning "oil press," was located at the foot of the Mount of Olives, about 300 yards (or 274 meters) east/northeast of Jerusalem and the Temple Mount. John's mention

---

[37] Many of the oldest and most highly regarded manuscripts omit verses 43 and 44, which strongly suggests that they are not part of the original text of Luke's Gospel.

of Jesus and his followers *entering* the garden may indicate that it was a walled garden (John 18:1).

It is now late in the night. Upon entering the garden, Jesus instructs his disciples to sit at a certain location while he goes farther on with his closest disciples: Peter, James, and John. The time for discussion and instruction is now over, and Jesus is filled with sorrow and distress in anticipation of the coming events. He shares his anguish with his closest human friends: "My soul is very sorrowful, even to death; remain here, and watch with me" (Matt. 26:38). Jesus's divinity did not eclipse his humanity (see John 11:35), and he keenly felt his need for human support and companionship during his final hours—it is no sign of weakness to want companionship and support before the evil face of death.

Jesus Prays

Going a little farther (a "stone's throw" according to Luke 22:41), Jesus engages in fervent personal prayer, crying out to his Father and imploring him to find another way—if there could be another way—yet ultimately submitting to God's will: "Abba, Father, all things are possible for you. Remove this cup from me. Yet not what I will, but what you will" (Mark 14:36). Jesus knows he is about to bear God's judgment for sin as a substitutionary sacrifice for the sins of the world. "Cup" was a common metaphor for God's righteous wrath poured out on sinners.[38] Jesus is about to drink this "cup" in the place of others; he is the only one who could.

In this Jesus's darkest hour, he models for his disciples and future believers the cost and necessity of full submission to the will of God. Submission is not always pleasant, and often painful, but it is always worth it. The author of Hebrews likely comments on these final hours of prayer when he writes, "In the days of his flesh, Jesus offered up prayers and supplications, with loud cries and tears, to him who was able to save him from death, and he was heard because of his reverence" (Heb. 5:7).

---

[38] Isaiah 51:17–23; Jeremiah 25:15–18; Lamentations 4:21; Ezekiel 23:31–33.

The Disciples Sleep

Taking a break from his prayer, Jesus turns to his disciples, only to find them sleeping. The only sources of human support and help during the hardest moments of his life prove to be unreliable. Even in this, Jesus is more concerned for their welfare than his own—he knows that they, too, must pray in order to be equipped to face the temptations and difficulties ahead. "Watch and pray that you may not enter into temptation. The spirit indeed is willing, but the flesh is weak" (Matt. 26:41). Jesus is not the only one about to be tested. Although Luke mentions this happening only once, Matthew and Mark provide the additional detail that this cycle was repeated three times. Each time Jesus left, he prayed, imploring God to find another way yet submitting himself to God's will, and each time he left, the disciples fell asleep. Mark also includes the detail that the disciples "did not know what to answer him" (Mark 14:40). They were likely ashamed and embarrassed, yet too tired to help themselves.

Luke provides two additional details. In the absence of human support, God did not leave Jesus alone but sent an angel to strengthen him (Luke 22:43; see also Matt. 4:11 where angels ministered to him in his weakness). This angelic support, however, could not remove the agony, and Luke describes Jesus's intense mental and physical condition by noting that "his sweat became like great drops of blood falling down to the ground" (Luke 22:44). The word "like" may indicate the use of metaphor, although Jesus could also have been experiencing hematidrosis, a rare medical condition in which the blood vessels burst under extreme anguish or physical stress and sweat mixes with blood. Jesus knew that he was about to make a costly sacrifice, and the only way out was to move forward.

When Jesus awakens the disciples the third time, he has evidently seen or heard the approaching mob and warns his disciples accordingly: the hour and betrayer are at hand—nap time is over. Jesus has prayed his heart out and is now ready to confidently face his coming death.

FRIDAY

APRIL 3, AD 33

THE BETRAYAL AND ARREST OF JESUS

Jesus is betrayed by Judas and arrested by the authorities (perhaps after midnight, early Friday morning).

MATTHEW 26:47-56

While he was still speaking, Judas came, one of the twelve, and with him a great crowd with swords and clubs, from the chief priests and the elders of the people.

Now the betrayer had given them a sign, saying,

"The one I will kiss is the man; seize him."

And he came up to Jesus at once and said,

"Greetings, Rabbi!"

And he kissed him.

Jesus said to him,

"Friend, do what you came to do."

Then they came up and laid hands on Jesus and seized him.

And behold, one of those who were with Jesus stretched out his hand and drew his sword and struck the servant of the high priest and cut off his ear.

Then Jesus said to him,

> "Put your sword back into its place.
>
>> For all who take the sword will perish by the sword.
>
> Do you think that I cannot appeal to my Father, and he will at once send me more than twelve legions of angels?
>
>> But how then should the Scriptures be fulfilled, that it must be so?"

At that hour Jesus said to the crowds,

> "Have you come out as against a robber, with swords and clubs to capture me?
>
> Day after day I sat in the temple teaching, and you did not seize me.
>
> But all this has taken place that the Scriptures of the prophets might be fulfilled."

Then all the disciples left him and fled.

MARK 14:43-52

And immediately, while he was still speaking, Judas came, one of the twelve, and with him a crowd with swords and clubs, from the chief priests and the scribes and the elders.

Now the betrayer had given them a sign, saying,

> "The one I will kiss is the man.
>
> Seize him and lead him away under guard."

And when he came, he went up to him at once and said,

> "Rabbi!"

And he kissed him.

And they laid hands on him and seized him.

But one of those who stood by drew his sword and struck the servant of the high priest and cut off his ear.

And Jesus said to them,

> "Have you come out as against a robber, with swords and clubs to capture me?
>
> Day after day I was with you in the temple teaching, and you did not seize me.
>
> But let the Scriptures be fulfilled."

And they all left him and fled.

And a young man followed him, with nothing but a linen cloth about his body.

And they seized him, but he left the linen cloth and ran away naked.

LUKE 22:47-53

While he was still speaking, there came a crowd, and the man called Judas, one of the twelve, was leading them. He drew near to Jesus to kiss him, but Jesus said to him,

> "Judas, would you betray the Son of Man with a kiss?"

And when those who were around him saw what would follow, they said,

> "Lord, shall we strike with the sword?"

And one of them struck the servant of the high priest and cut off his right ear.

But Jesus said,

> "No more of this!"

And he touched his ear and healed him.

Then Jesus said to the chief priests and officers of the temple and elders, who had come out against him,

"Have you come out as against a robber, with swords and clubs?

When I was with you day after day in the temple, you did not lay hands on me.

But this is your hour, and the power of darkness."

JOHN 18:2-12

Now Judas, who betrayed him, also knew the place, for Jesus often met there with his disciples. So Judas, having procured a band of soldiers and some officers from the chief priests and the Pharisees, went there with lanterns and torches and weapons.

Then Jesus, knowing all that would happen to him, came forward and said to them,

"Whom do you seek?"

They answered him,

"Jesus of Nazareth."

Jesus said to them,

"I am he."

Judas, who betrayed him, was standing with them.

When Jesus said to them,

"I am he,"

they drew back and fell to the ground.

So he asked them again,

"Whom do you seek?"

And they said,

"Jesus of Nazareth."

Jesus answered,

"I told you that I am he.

So, if you seek me, let these men go."

This was to fulfill the word that he had spoken:

"Of those whom you gave me I have lost not one."

Then Simon Peter, having a sword, drew it and struck the high priest's servant and cut off his right ear.

(The servant's name was Malchus.)

So Jesus said to Peter,

"Put your sword into its sheath; shall I not drink the cup that the Father has given me?"

So the band of soldiers and their captain and the officers of the Jews arrested Jesus and bound him.

COMMENTARY

The Setting

The scene is the garden of Gethsemane—a place Judas knew because Jesus often met there with his disciples.[1] The time was most likely after midnight, early Friday morning. Judas's appearance ominously signals Jesus's imminent demise. Matthew, Mark, and Luke all draw attention to the fact that Judas was "one of the twelve."[2] One can almost discern a mixture of disgust and incredulity in the evangelists' account: one of the Twelve, Jesus's inner circle, has treacherously turned against him and betrayed his Master.

The "Great Crowd"

Judas leads a crowd—Matthew even speaks of a "great crowd"[3]— with swords and clubs, sent from the chief priests, the scribes, and the elders (i.e., the Jewish ruling council, the Sanhedrin; details

[1] John 18:2.
[2] Matthew 26:47; Mark 14:43; Luke 22:47.
[3] Matthew 26:47.

omitted by Luke). Judas has procured a band of soldiers (Roman guards) and some officers from the chief priests and the Pharisees (mentioned here only by John), who arrive with lanterns and torches—indicating the late night hour—and a variety of weapons.[4] One cannot help but be struck by the almost comical overkill of the scene: did it really take a "great crowd" of people, armed with swords, clubs, and perhaps other weapons, to take charge of Jesus? This stands in sharp contrast to the harmless, peaceful, and nonaggressive conduct of Jesus recounted in all the Gospels during his three-year earthly ministry (though see the incident involving Peter below).

Judas's Kiss

In the next scene, we are told that Judas had arranged with those who were with him that he would identify Jesus—the one to be arrested—with a kiss, the famous "Judas kiss." Once again, the irony is palpable. While normally a kiss signified deep love and affection, in the present case it marks Judas's betrayal of Jesus— the ultimate treachery. So after greeting Jesus with the customary address of "rabbi" (Aramaic for "teacher"),[5] Judas kisses his Master, consummating the betrayal. As Luke records, Jesus asks, "Judas, would you betray the Son of Man with a kiss?" (22:48). This is at once a gentle rebuke and a deeply felt acknowledgment of the unspeakable tragedy and travesty of justice that are about to unfold.

Jesus Takes Charge

Several of the evangelists point out that at his arrest, Jesus is no passive victim but actively and repeatedly takes the initiative. According to Matthew, Jesus says to Judas, "Friend, do what you came to do."[6] And John, emphasizing that Jesus knows all that is about to happen to him, notes how Jesus steps forward and asks the crowd, "Whom do you seek?" When they answer, "Jesus of Nazareth,"

---

[4] John 18:3.
[5] Matthew 26:49; Mark 14:45.
[6] Matthew 26:50.

Jesus replies, "I am he," a phrase reminiscent of "I AM," one of the Old Testament names for God (Ex. 3:14). When Jesus reiterates that he is the one they had come for, the soldiers draw back and fall to the ground, similar to the customary response to a theophany (a manifestation of God's presence; e.g., Ex. 3:1–6; 19:16–24). Jesus tells the soldiers to go ahead and arrest him and to let his followers go—not only an exceedingly noble gesture of the "good shepherd" protecting his "sheep" but also a deliberate act fulfilling Scripture concerning Jesus's preservation of all those whom the Father had given him.[7] Thus even when sinners take charge of Jesus to arrest him, the evangelists make clear that ultimately Jesus is still very much in charge.

Peter Cuts Off Malchus's Ear

At this, the evangelists record that one of the disciples—Peter—briefly seeks to resist arrest by cutting off the right ear of the high priest's servant (a man by the name of Malchus).[8] But Jesus sharply rebukes Peter, noting that those who take the sword will perish by the sword.[9] For his part, Jesus reaffirms that he is determined to "drink the cup that the Father has given [him]."[10] ("The cup" often in the Bible serves as a symbol of divine judgment or wrath.) He also notes that he could appeal to the Father, who would at once send him more than twelve legions (12 x 6,000) of angels.[11] And he touches the servant's ear and miraculously heals him.

Jesus a Robber?

Then Jesus draws attention to the irony of having a large crowd armed with weapons come to arrest him: "Have you come out as against a robber, with swords and clubs?"[12] As Jesus notes, such

---

[7] John 18:4–9.
[8] Note that only John identifies Peter and Malchus by name (John 18:10–11).
[9] Matthew 26:52.
[10] John 18:11.
[11] Matthew 26:53. A typical legion was made up of 5,120 legionaries plus a large number of camp followers, servants, and slaves. Including the auxiliaries, it could contain as many as six thousand fighting men.
[12] Matthew 26:55; Mark 14:48.

stealth and force were completely unnecessary, for he had been teaching in the temple area day after day. The soldiers' coming by night and their covert operation against a patently innocent man signal the truth of Jesus's statement: "But this is your hour, and the power of darkness."[13] Satan sought to destroy the Messiah and Son of God in one frontal assault on the one who had come to set God's people free. At this, all the disciples leave Jesus and flee, including a young man who runs away naked, eluding the soldiers who try to seize him.[14]

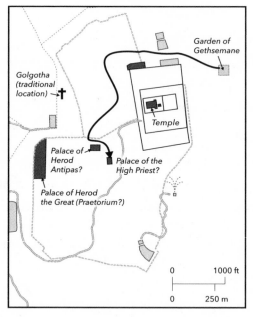

**From the Garden of Gethsemane
to the Palace of the High Priest**

---

[13] Luke 22:53.
[14] Mark 14:51–52. The identity of the young man is unknown. Some speculate it is Mark, the author of the Gospel.

THE JEWISH TRIAL OF JESUS (PHASE 1): INFORMAL

Jesus has an informal hearing before Annas (former high priest and Caiaphas's father-in-law).

JOHN 18:13-14, 19-24

First they led him to Annas, for he was the father-in-law of Caiaphas, who was high priest that year. It was Caiaphas who had advised the Jews that it would be expedient that one man should die for the people. . . .

The high priest [i.e., Annas] then questioned Jesus about his disciples and his teaching.

Jesus answered him,

> "I have spoken openly to the world.
>
> I have always taught in synagogues and in the temple, where all Jews come together.
>
> I have said nothing in secret.
>
> Why do you ask me?
>
> Ask those who have heard me what I said to them; they know what I said."

When he had said these things, one of the officers standing by struck Jesus with his hand, saying,

> "Is that how you answer the high priest?"

Jesus answered him,

> "If what I said is wrong, bear witness about the wrong;
>
> but if what I said is right, why do you strike me?"

Annas then sent him bound to Caiaphas the high priest.

COMMENTARY

John alone includes this account of a brief hearing before Annas, the former high priest and father-in-law of the present high priest,

Caiaphas. Annas exercised a great deal of authority and power even though he was not the reigning high priest.[15] Since the mob brought Jesus to Annas first, Annas may have been the one who had masterminded Jesus's arrest after Judas had approached the chief priests concerning his betrayal. By the time of this initial hearing, it would likely have been very early Friday morning.

Annas questions Jesus about his teaching and his disciples, indicating a concern with both theological and political issues. Jesus responds by making it clear that he has never concealed his teaching or other activities and has done everything in the public eye (John 18:20). He has nothing to hide, no private agenda lurks behind his public teaching, and his previous words and actions prove his innocence. Annas should question those who had heard Jesus's teaching (John 18:21). It seems reasonable to suppose that Jesus knew that Annas was not really concerned with truth at this point—Annas knew quite well what Jesus had been saying and teaching and was simply looking for grounds to propose the death sentence.

An officer standing nearby violently strikes Jesus for his "disrespectful" answer, very likely on the basis of Exodus 22:28, which states: "You shall not revile God, nor curse a ruler of your people." Jesus maintains his innocence and denies any wrongdoing. He insists that his accusers specify the wrong he allegedly has committed. If they cannot substantiate the charges, why was he struck (John 18:23)?

Annas, apparently frustrated with Jesus's refusal to answer his questions, sends him bound to his son-in-law, Caiaphas the high priest. This first stage of Jesus's trial functions as an informal hearing in preparation for a more formal hearing before a fuller contingent of the Sanhedrin. Before charges can be brought against Jesus before the Roman governor, the charges must be formally confirmed by Caiaphas, who is also head of the Jewish high court. Jesus possibly could have talked his way out of trouble at this stage

---

[15] Annas and Caiaphas had a close relationship of shared power and influence. Luke 3:2 notes that John came baptizing "during the high priesthood of Annas and Caiaphas," and John 18:19, 22, 24 describe both Annas and Caiaphas as "high priest." Annas was officially high priest during AD 6–15, but he continued to exercise considerable influence since as many as five of his sons, in addition to his son-in-law Caiaphas, subsequently served as high priest.

if he had repented of his teaching and submitted to Annas's and Caiaphas's religious authority. But Jesus's prayer in the garden confirmed his resolve and established his course—there would be no turning back from the fate ahead of him. He would die, according to the will of God, for the sins of God's people. The Jewish leaders, for their part, had no real concern for justice or fairness—they wanted Jesus dead and were willing to do whatever it took to get him out of the way.

THE JEWISH TRIAL OF JESUS (PHASE 2): MORE FORMAL

Jesus stands trial before Caiaphas and part of the Sanhedrin.

MATTHEW 26:57, 59-68

Then those who had seized Jesus led him to Caiaphas the high priest, where the scribes and the elders had gathered. . . .

Now the chief priests and the whole council were seeking false testimony against Jesus that they might put him to death, but they found none, though many false witnesses came forward. At last two came forward and said,

> "This man said,
>
> > 'I am able to destroy the temple of God, and to rebuild it in three days.'"

And the high priest stood up and said,

> "Have you no answer to make?
>
> What is it that these men testify against you?"

But Jesus remained silent.

And the high priest said to him,

> "I adjure you by the living God, tell us if you are the Christ, the Son of God."

Jesus said to him,

> "You have said so.

> But I tell you, from now on you will see the Son of Man seated at the right hand of Power and coming on the clouds of heaven."

Then the high priest tore his robes and said,

> "He has uttered blasphemy.

> What further witnesses do we need?

> You have now heard his blasphemy.

> What is your judgment?"

They answered,

> "He deserves death."

Then they spit in his face and struck him.

And some slapped him, saying,

> "Prophesy to us, you Christ!

> Who is it that struck you?"

MARK 14:53, 55-65

And they led Jesus to the high priest.

And all the chief priests and the elders and the scribes came together. . . .

Now the chief priests and the whole council were seeking testimony against Jesus to put him to death, but they found none. For many bore false witness against him, but their testimony did not agree.

And some stood up and bore false witness against him, saying,

> "We heard him say,

'I will destroy this temple that is made with hands, and in three days I will build another, not made with hands.'"

Yet even about this their testimony did not agree.

And the high priest stood up in the midst and asked Jesus,

> "Have you no answer to make?
>
> What is it that these men testify against you?"

But he remained silent and made no answer.

Again the high priest asked him,

> "Are you the Christ, the Son of the Blessed?"

And Jesus said,

> "I am, and you will see the Son of Man seated at the right hand of Power, and coming with the clouds of heaven."

And the high priest tore his garments and said,

> "What further witnesses do we need?
>
> You have heard his blasphemy.
>
> What is your decision?"

And they all condemned him as deserving death.

And some began to spit on him and to cover his face and to strike him, saying to him,

> "Prophesy!"

And the guards received him with blows.

LUKE 22:63–71

Now the men who were holding Jesus in custody were mocking him as they beat him. They also blindfolded him and kept asking him,

> "Prophesy! Who is it that struck you?"

And they said many other things against him, blaspheming him.

When day came, the assembly of the elders of the people gathered together, both chief priests and scribes. And they led him away to their council, and they said,

> "If you are the Christ, tell us."

But he said to them,

> "If I tell you, you will not believe, and if I ask you, you will not answer.

> But from now on the Son of Man shall be seated at the right hand of the power of God."

So they all said,

> "Are you the Son of God, then?"

And he said to them,

> "You say that I am."

Then they said,

> "What further testimony do we need?

We have heard it ourselves from his own lips."

COMMENTARY

The Council Gathers

As the long, dark morning progresses, word is quickly sent to the Jewish religious leadership—the chief priests, elders, and scribes—informing them of Jesus's capture and calling them to gather quickly at Caiaphas's house for a speedy trial. Caiaphas's residence was likely a mansion overlooking the temple complex in Jerusalem's upper city. The reference here to the "whole council" likely refers to a quorum (at least twenty-three members) and does not necessarily indicate that every single one of the Sanhedrin's members had gathered as of yet. Members likely continued arriving until the final verdict was declared shortly after sunrise.

Accusations and Silence

The Jewish leaders hurry to expedite the trial and arrive at the death sentence before the day progresses and news of Jesus's arrest can spread among the masses of Passover pilgrims. They will be in a much stronger position to spin the story and engage in damage control of popular opinion once a sentence has been reached. In their haste to proceed with the trial, they are not particularly careful in their selection of witnesses and therefore can only come up with contradictory accounts. No charges could stick apart from the agreement of at least two witnesses, and clearly the witnesses whose testimony the Jewish leaders have solicited are not committed to the truth.[16] Matthew describes them from the start as "false witnesses."

The most serious charge Jesus's accusers are able to produce is his statement, "Destroy this temple, and in three days I will raise it up" (John 2:19–21). Jesus was speaking of the "temple" of his body and was presenting himself as the replacement of the physical temple, which would soon be destroyed by the Romans. Jesus will soon be the person through whom God's people have complete and unhindered access to God. His words, however, were easily misinterpreted and twisted ("I will destroy this temple," Mark 14:58) as a threat against the physical temple—as if Jesus somehow wanted to lead an armed mob to destroy the physical temple! Even with regard to this charge, however, the testimony of Jesus's accusers does not agree (Mark 14:59).

Jesus responds to these claims with utter silence, for he knows that the outcome of the proceedings against him is already determined, and there is nothing he can say that will not subsequently be twisted and used against him. The court has already made up its mind and is simply looking for the smallest grounds for the death sentence. Jesus's silence also fulfills the prophecy made concerning the suffering servant in Isaiah: "He was oppressed, and he was afflicted, yet he opened not his mouth; like a lamb that is led to the slaughter, and like a sheep that before its shearers is silent,

---

[16] Since these witnesses could not agree on a coherent story, their testimony could not be used in a formal charge (see Deut. 17:6).

so he opened not his mouth" (Isa. 53:7). Jesus's silence places full responsibility upon his accusers for the outcome of the trial.

Jesus's Claim

The high priest was apparently getting impatient with the progress of the trial and Jesus's refusal to answer the various false witnesses. He asks Jesus directly whether he is the Christ, the Son of God.[17] An affirmative answer will give Caiaphas a legitimate basis for requesting the death penalty from Pontius Pilate: insurrection and treason. This was the only question that really mattered, and Jesus's answer does not disappoint: not only does Jesus break his silence with an affirmative answer, but also he proceeds to apply both Daniel 7:13–14 and Psalm 110:1–2 to himself. He himself is the divine Son of Man who will sit at Yahweh's right hand and come on the clouds to receive his universal eternal kingdom.

This affirmation seals Jesus's death on both theological and political grounds. Theologically, Jesus has blasphemed by claiming to be the Son of God—this was completely unacceptable to the Jewish leadership. Politically, Jesus has claimed to be the one who will come as God's agent to receive cosmic kingship—this was unacceptable to the Romans who recognized only one emperor. The Sanhedrin now has what they want. Jesus has made a clear, self-incriminating statement in front of many witnesses that expresses his unique divine relationship to Yahweh and declares his intentions to overthrow the Romans, and all earthly kingdoms, and establish God's kingdom on earth. Ironically, this is exactly what many first-century Jews hoped and longed for, but the reigning Jewish leadership has already made up their minds that Jesus is not the one. After all, how could Jesus be God's Messiah when he did not support the currently established temple leadership?

Following Jesus's startling and unexpected declaration, the

---

[17] Matthew 26:63; Mark 14:61; Luke 22:67. Luke's account (Luke 22:63–71) summarizes and conflates all three phases of the Jewish trial around this one question and Jesus's answer, indicating that this was the central issue and charge from the point of view of Luke and his intended readers. The question of Jesus's messianic identity hung over his entire public ministry. On the one hand, his words and actions fit messianic expectations, but he never publicly claimed to be the Messiah (John 10:24; see also his private instructions to his disciples in Matt. 16:20; Mark 8:30).

high priest tears his robes and puts an end to further witnesses: "What further witnesses do we need?"[18] High priests were prohibited from engaging in the symbolic action of tearing one's clothes (Lev. 10:6; 21:10), but Jesus's "blasphemous" answer produces an immediate, vehement response with no regard for such technicalities: "And they all condemned him as deserving death."[19] Despite Jesus's death sentence by the Sanhedrin, the Jews were not allowed to execute individuals under Roman rule.[20] The Romans permitted the Jews a degree of judicial freedom in regard to their own cases but reserved the final say in cases of capital punishment. Jesus will stand trial for his life before the Roman governor Pontius Pilate.

The Beatings Begin

Although the Jewish leaders needed to wait until sunrise on Friday to grant a formal Jewish verdict and receive approval from the Roman governor, the end result was not in doubt, and the mocking and abuse began. Surrounding guards, probably leaders of the temple police, begin to spit on Jesus and strike him. This physical abuse brought about the fulfillment of Isaiah's prophecies: "His appearance was so marred, beyond human semblance, and his form beyond that of the children of mankind" (Isa. 52:14); and "I gave my back to those who strike, and my cheeks to those who pull out the beard; I hid not my face from disgrace and spitting" (Isa. 50:6).

The guards mock his claim to be God's Messiah by covering his eyes, striking him, and asking him to prophesy concerning the identity of the one who struck him.[21] They address him as "Christ" in mockery, not faith. Luke notes that they blasphemed him by saying many other things against him.[22] This mockery and physical abuse is just a foretaste of what Jesus will soon experience at the hands of Roman soldiers.

———————————•◦•———————————

---

18 Matthew 26:65; Mark 14:63; Luke 22:71.
19 Mark 14:64; see also Matthew 26:66.
20 See John 18:31.
21 Matthew 26:68; Mark 14:65; Luke 22:64.
22 Luke 22:65.

PETER DENIES JESUS

As predicted, Peter denies Jesus and the rooster crows.

MATTHEW 26:58, 69-75

And Peter was following him at a distance, as far as the courtyard of the high priest, and going inside he sat with the guards to see the end. . . .

Now Peter was sitting outside in the courtyard.

And a servant girl came up to him and said,

"You also were with Jesus the Galilean."

But he denied it before them all, saying,

"I do not know what you mean."

And when he went out to the entrance, another servant girl saw him, and she said to the bystanders,

"This man was with Jesus of Nazareth."

And again he denied it with an oath:

"I do not know the man."

After a little while the bystanders came up and said to Peter,

"Certainly you too are one of them, for your accent betrays you."

Then he began to invoke a curse on himself and to swear,

"I do not know the man."

And immediately the rooster crowed.

And Peter remembered the saying of Jesus,

"Before the rooster crows, you will deny me three times."

And he went out and wept bitterly.

MARK 14:54, 66-72

Peter had followed him at a distance, right into the courtyard of the high priest.

And he was sitting with the guards and warming himself at the fire. . . .

And as Peter was below in the courtyard, one of the servant girls of the high priest came, and seeing Peter warming himself, she looked at him and said,

"You also were with the Nazarene, Jesus."

But he denied it, saying,

"I neither know nor understand what you mean."

And he went out into the gateway and the rooster crowed. And the servant girl saw him and began again to say to the bystanders,

"This man is one of them."

But again he denied it.

And after a little while the bystanders again said to Peter,

"Certainly you are one of them, for you are a Galilean."

But he began to invoke a curse on himself and to swear,

"I do not know this man of whom you speak."

And immediately the rooster crowed a second time.

And Peter remembered how Jesus had said to him,

"Before the rooster crows twice, you will deny me three times."

And he broke down and wept.

LUKE 22:54b-62

. . . and Peter was following at a distance.

And when they had kindled a fire in the middle of the courtyard and sat down together, Peter sat down among them.

Then a servant girl, seeing him as he sat in the light and looking closely at him, said,

"This man also was with him."

But he denied it, saying,

"Woman, I do not know him."

And a little later someone else saw him and said,

"You also are one of them."

But Peter said,

"Man, I am not."

And after an interval of about an hour still another insisted, saying,

"Certainly this man also was with him, for he too is a Galilean."

But Peter said,

"Man, I do not know what you are talking about."

And immediately, while he was still speaking, the rooster crowed.

And the Lord turned and looked at Peter.

And Peter remembered the saying of the Lord, how he had said to him,

"Before the rooster crows today, you will deny me three times."

And he went out and wept bitterly.

JOHN 18:15-18, 25-27

Simon Peter followed Jesus, and so did another disciple.

Since that disciple was known to the high priest, he entered with Jesus into the courtyard of the high priest, but Peter stood outside at the door.

So the other disciple, who was known to the high priest, went out and spoke to the servant girl who kept watch at the door, and brought Peter in.

The servant girl at the door said to Peter,

"You also are not one of this man's disciples, are you?"

He said,

"I am not."

Now the servants and officers had made a charcoal fire, because it was cold, and they were standing and warming themselves.

Peter also was with them, standing and warming himself. . . .

Now Simon Peter was standing and warming himself.

So they said to him,

"You also are not one of his disciples, are you?"

He denied it and said,

"I am not."

One of the servants of the high priest, a relative of the man whose ear Peter had cut off, asked,

"Did I not see you in the garden with him?"

Peter again denied it, and at once a rooster crowed.

COMMENTARY

Peter's denial of Jesus stands as one of the most poignant and memorable events that transpired during Jesus's final day. One of Jesus's closest friends, a man who hours earlier had sworn to stand by Jesus no matter what the sacrifice or cost, denies even knowing Jesus and abandons him in his darkest hour. Pathos drips from the Gospel accounts—the tragedy is palpable, and Peter leaves the scene a broken man.

Initial Loyalty

At first, Peter seems to be making good on his earlier pledges of loyalty. When all the other disciples except one, "[an]other disciple" (likely John), abandon Jesus and flee for their lives in fear, Peter follows and gets as close as he possibly can to the scene of the Jewish trial.[23] John describes how Peter gained access to the courtyard of the high priest. John is somehow known to the high priest and easily gains entrance for himself. When John notices that Peter is loitering outside the courtyard, he speaks to the servant girl who is watching the door and convinces her to let Peter in as well.

Peter and John are both putting their lives on the line at this point. Their leader is on trial for his life and is being explicitly questioned by Annas about his disciples (John 18:19).[24] So far, Peter is risking his life to stay near his leader. Apparently, John is able to get inside the house while Peter remains in the courtyard and warms himself near a charcoal fire with servants, officers, and other bystanders. He is determined to stay near Jesus until the end (Matt. 26:58).

Suspicions and Denial

Peter was obviously hoping to blend in with the crowds of people and observe the proceedings from anonymous safety. Trouble begins when the servant girl who had given Peter entrance at the door approaches and confronts Peter: "You also were with Jesus the Galilean."[25] She had apparently seen Peter with Jesus at some point in the past week of Jesus's public ministry. Peter immediately denies having known Jesus "before them all" (Matt. 26:70).

A little later, another servant girl begins to say the same thing, and she along with the bystanders again ask Peter if he is one of Jesus's disciples.[26] This time he denies acquaintance with Jesus by an oath.[27] The oath emphasizes to those around that he certainly is not one of Jesus's disciples.

---

[23] Matthew 26:58; Mark 14:54; Luke 22:54–55; John 18:15–16. Luke places Peter's denial before phase 2 of the Jewish trial, Matthew and Mark place it after phase 2, and John divides it into two sections before and after phase 1 of the Jewish trial. These differences are not contradictions but the constraints of narrative storytelling: the time span of Peter's denials parallels the first two stages of Jesus's Jewish trial, so each narrator had to place it either before or after. The events took place simultaneously.

[24] Jesus refused to answer Annas's question about his disciples, likely protecting them from immediate arrest and future suspicion and harassment (John 18:20–21).

[25] Matthew 26:69; see also Mark 14:66–67; Luke 22:56; John 18:17.

[26] Matthew 26:71; Mark 14:69; Luke 22:58; John 18:25.

[27] Matthew 26:72. Jesus had taught that oaths should not be taken (Matt. 5:33–37). Among his followers, no oaths were needed—every word should be truthful.

A third time, about an hour later, according to Luke, the bystanders again question Peter's relationship to Jesus. John mentions that a relative of Malchus (the man whose ear Peter had cut off) led this round of questioning (John 18:26). Peter's Galilean accent gives him away and makes clear to the bystanders that he is from Galilee. Putting two and two together, they conclude that he is, after all, very likely one of Jesus's followers. At this point, Peter is pretty scared. His plan to blend in with the crowd and to observe the proceedings from anonymous safety have completely failed, and the bystanders know he has been lying about his relationship with Jesus. How can he convince them? In desperation, Peter resorts to the most drastic affirmation of truth he can think of—he calls down a curse on himself and solemnly swears that he does not know Jesus.[28] Such an emphatic curse likely convinced some of the bystanders—it was a very serious matter to call down God's wrath upon oneself.

What would have happened if Peter had not denied Jesus and had openly acknowledged his allegiance to the accused? He would very likely have been detained for questioning and been harassed. It was not likely that he would have lost his life—it was hard enough for the Jewish leaders to get Pilate to sentence Jesus to death, much less one of Jesus's followers. On the other hand, Peter's act of violence in the garden of Gethsemane (cutting off Malchus's ear) may have led to harsher consequences—at least at this point he had good reasons to suspect that he was in danger of imprisonment or death. What is more, unlike Jesus, Peter did not have the protection of widespread popular favor. But in stark contrast to the example of Jesus, Peter chose the path of expedience instead of faithfulness, being paralyzed by the fear of man rather than the fear of the Lord.

The Rooster Crows

Immediately following Peter's third denial the rooster crows.[29] Luke notes that Jesus at this time turned and looked at him—

---

[28] Matthew 26:74; Mark 14:71.
[29] Mark mentions that the rooster had already crowed between the first and second denial and that Jesus had prophesied that the rooster would crow twice before Peter denied him three times. Far from representing a contradiction, this variation rather illustrates the Gospel authors'

implying eye contact. Jesus may have looked out a window. Or perhaps he was being moved from one location to another within the residence and gained sight of the courtyard.[30] In either case, Jesus's look—likely less of a glare and more of a serious look filled with sadness and compassion—triggers Peter's memory. In all the excitement and danger of the morning, he has forgotten about Jesus's earlier prophecy, that he was going to deny Jesus three times before the rooster crowed that night—a prediction that Peter had vehemently denied, even rebuked.

Upon remembering Jesus's words, Peter rapidly leaves the courtyard, finds his way into the safety of the dark, maze-like streets of Jerusalem, and weeps bitterly. Everything he thought he knew about himself, all his self-confidence and belief in his undying loyalty to his Master, has been shattered and lies in utter ruins. He sees himself as a failure, a liar, a traitor, and one who has just invoked God's wrath upon himself in denying the Messiah just to save his own skin. Perhaps he recalled Jesus's earlier words: "Whoever denies me before men, I also will deny before my Father who is in heaven."[31] Not only has he betrayed and denied the man he had trusted and followed for the past three years, leaving him to face his accusers and die alone, but also he has incriminated himself before God's judgment seat by uttering his curse and oath.

---

freedom to include different levels of detail. Mark provides the most detail, while the others note, in more general terms, that at the crowing of a rooster, Peter recalled Jesus's words, broke down, and fled the scene.

[30] Between 1973–1974 six Herodian villas were excavated in Jerusalem (under the leadership of Nahman Avigad) and then restored from 1985–1987 (under the supervision of Leen Ritmeyer). One of the buildings, known as the Palatial Mansion (or Herodian Mansion), was undoubtedly used by the temple priests. It was located just opposite the southwest corner of the Temple Mount and was unusually large, with a footprint of 6,500 square feet (600 m2). Its usable living space was twice that size. Its size, location, ornamentation, and four ritual baths—combined with evidence of a large fire—have led to a possible identification as the palace of Annas the high priest, which had been burned in AD 70 (Josephus, *War* 2:426). The plan of the palace was designed around a central courtyard. There is a spot in the southwest corner of the courtyard (near the entrance/exit) that would allow someone such as Peter to look directly through the window of the large reception hall, which measured 33 feet by 21 feet (11 m by 6.5 m). The mansion was built into a slope descending to the east. Because the entrance was higher than the courtyard, Peter would have descended stairs to reach the courtyard, which fits with Mark's comment that Peter was "below in the courtyard" (Mark 14:66). For more details, see the following interview: http://thegospelcoalition.org/blogs/justintaylor/2012/08/28/is-this-the-high-priestly-palace-where-jesus-stood-trial/.

[31] Matthew 10:33; see also Mark 8:38; Luke 12:9.

Peter's self-inflicted emotional and spiritual anguish sharply contrasts with the physical and emotional suffering to which Jesus was subjected at the same time. Peter knew that his actions had placed him irrevocably (or so he thought) under God's wrath, while Jesus knew that he must soon experience the full outpouring of God's wrath so that Peter, and all others who placed their faith in Jesus, would not have to do the same.

THE JEWISH TRIAL OF JESUS (PHASE 3): THE FINAL VERDICT

After sunrise on Friday, the final consultation of the full Sanhedrin condemns Jesus to death and sends him to Pilate.

MATTHEW 27:1-2

When morning came, all the chief priests and the elders of the people took counsel against Jesus to put him to death.

And they bound him and led him away and delivered him over to Pilate the governor.

MARK 15:1

And as soon as it was morning, the chief priests held a consultation with the elders and scribes and the whole council.

And they bound Jesus and led him away and delivered him over to Pilate.

COMMENTARY

The Gospel authors pass over the final verdict of the Jewish trial in relative brevity. The most powerful members of the council had already reached their verdict—there was no doubt after Jesus's christological confession and the high priest's dramatic tearing of his robes that Jesus was worthy of death. The formal verdict only requires the advent of sunrise and a quorum of the Sanhedrin. This final judgment possesses an air of legality that the earlier verdict lacked. The appearance of legality, in turn, is essential if the Jewish leaders are to win the battle for public opinion.

The Jewish leaders waste no time in passing the verdict and in bringing their charges against Jesus before Pilate. It is important for them to get this matter taken care of as soon as possible in order to avoid any civil disturbance at the Passover and for them to be able to take part in the normal rituals of the festival. The trial is over just as quickly as it had begun, and Jesus's fate is now in the hands of the Roman governor Pontius Pilate.

From the Sanhedrin to Pontius Pilate

JUDAS HANGS HIMSELF

Judas changes his mind, returns the silver, and hangs himself.

MATTHEW 27:3-10

Then when Judas, his betrayer, saw that Jesus was condemned, he changed his mind and brought back the thirty pieces of silver to the chief priests and the elders, saying,

"I have sinned by betraying innocent blood."

They said,

"What is that to us? See to it yourself."

And throwing down the pieces of silver into the temple, he departed, and he went and hanged himself. But the chief priests, taking the pieces of silver, said,

"It is not lawful to put them into the treasury, since it is blood money."

So they took counsel and bought with them the potter's field as a burial place for strangers. Therefore that field has been called the Field of Blood to this day. Then was fulfilled what had been spoken by the prophet Jeremiah, saying,

"And they took the thirty pieces of silver, the price of him on whom a price had been set by some of the sons of Israel, and they gave them for the potter's field, as the Lord directed me." [Jer. 19:1–14; Zech. 11:11–13]

COMMENTARY

Matthew alone records the fate of Judas, Jesus's betrayer. As soon as Judas sees that Jesus is condemned and realizes that his execution is a virtual certainty, he changes his mind, brings the money back, and tries to defend Jesus with his confession: "I have sinned by betraying innocent blood."[32] This defense was a day late and a shekel short;

---

[32] Matthew 27:4.

there was nothing Judas could do to reverse the damage he had done. The die had been cast. God may be a God of second chances (see, for example, Peter's restoration upon repentance), but in Judas's case at least, the consequences of his betrayal were irreversible. All of Judas's remorse was not going to undo the part he had played in Jesus's opponents' wicked scheme. They had used him, and he had given them exactly what they wanted, right when they needed it.

In fact, the chief priests and elders care nothing for Judas, his guilt, or his change of heart. There is no concern on their part for truth, innocence, or repentance. Judas responds to their callousness by throwing the thirty pieces of silver—about four months' wages for a laborer—onto the floor of the temple. Was he attempting to atone for his actions? He leaves the scene and proceeds to hang himself.[33] Judas's suicide and Jesus's comments about him in John 17:12 ("not one of [the disciples] has been lost except the son of destruction") indicate that his change of mind did not result in saving repentance. He felt guilt and remorse, but instead of turning to God to ask for forgiveness in humility and repentance as Jesus had taught in the parable of the prodigal son (Luke 15:11–24), Judas took his own life.[34]

The chief priests, for their part, are left with a bit of a problem. What should they do with the money? They cannot put it into the temple treasury, because it is blood money.[35] They finally decide to purchase a field to use as a burial place for strangers—a kind of John and Jane Doe public cemetery. Unknowingly, their actions fulfill a prophecy drawn from Jeremiah 19:1–14 and Zechariah 11:11–13. Jeremiah is mentioned as the author of the prophecy most likely because he was the more prominent prophet of the two.[36]

---

[33] The account of Judas's death in Acts 1:18–19 is complementary. Acts 1:18 notes that Judas acquired a field (indirectly, through the agency of the chief priests). The fall of Judas's body and the gruesome details recorded in Acts 1:18 could be due either to his body falling shortly after death from the rope or branch or to his body being left hanging for a period long enough to decay and decompose, eventually falling down and bursting open. The accounts in Matthew and Acts focus on different aspects and details of the event.

[34] The reality of 2 Corinthians 7:10 is a sad but fitting analysis of Judas's situation: "Godly grief produces a repentance that leads to salvation without regret, whereas worldly grief produces death."

[35] The chief priests were likely following the commands found in Deuteronomy 23:18.

[36] This is similar to how Mark combines words from Isaiah (Isa. 40:3) and Malachi (Mal. 3:1) in Mark 1:2 while citing only Isaiah as the more popular prophet. There is precedent for this procedure in rabbinic practice as well.

Interpreters have speculated concerning Judas's motives. Was he simply greedy and opportunistic? John notes that Judas was a thief and often stole from Jesus's and the disciples' common purse (John 12:6). Was he disillusioned with Jesus when he realized that Jesus was not going to be the militaristic Messiah he was looking for? Did he hope that his betrayal would force Jesus's hand and cause Jesus to overthrow the present Jewish leadership and the Romans? The Gospel writers do not inform us of his motives apart from noting Satan's involvement in his actions.[37] Satan did not take complete possession of Judas but likely exploited his weaknesses with increased temptation. At the same time, Satan's involvement does not remove Judas's complicity and responsibility for the betrayal.

THE ROMAN TRIAL OF JESUS (PHASE 1): PILATE

Pontius Pilate questions Jesus and sends him to Herod Antipas.

MATTHEW 27:11-14

Now Jesus stood before the governor, and the governor asked him,

"Are you the King of the Jews?"

Jesus said,

"You have said so."

But when he was accused by the chief priests and elders, he gave no answer.

Then Pilate said to him,

"Do you not hear how many things they testify against you?"

But he gave him no answer, not even to a single charge, so that the governor was greatly amazed.

---

[37] Luke 22:3; John 13:2, 27.

MARK 15:2-5

And Pilate asked him,

> "Are you the King of the Jews?"

And he answered him,

> "You have said so."

And the chief priests accused him of many things.

And Pilate again asked him,

> "Have you no answer to make? See how many charges they bring against you."

But Jesus made no further answer, so that Pilate was amazed.

LUKE 23:1-7

Then the whole company of them arose and brought him before Pilate. And they began to accuse him, saying,

> "We found this man misleading our nation and forbidding us to give tribute to Caesar, and saying that he himself is Christ, a king."

And Pilate asked him,

> "Are you the King of the Jews?"

And he answered him,

> "You have said so."

Then Pilate said to the chief priests and the crowds,

> "I find no guilt in this man."

But they were urgent, saying,

> "He stirs up the people, teaching throughout all Judea, from Galilee even to this place."

When Pilate heard this, he asked whether the man was a Galilean.

And when he learned that he belonged to Herod's jurisdiction, he sent him over to Herod, who was himself in Jerusalem at that time.

JOHN 18:28-38

Then they led Jesus from the house of Caiaphas to the governor's headquarters. It was early morning. They themselves did not enter the governor's headquarters, so that they would not be defiled, but could eat the Passover. So Pilate went outside to them and said,

"What accusation do you bring against this man?"

They answered him,

"If this man were not doing evil, we would not have delivered him over to you."

Pilate said to them,

"Take him yourselves and judge him by your own law."

The Jews said to him,

"It is not lawful for us to put anyone to death."

This was to fulfill the word that Jesus had spoken to show by what kind of death he was going to die.

So Pilate entered his headquarters again and called Jesus and said to him,

"Are you the King of the Jews?"

Jesus answered,

"Do you say this of your own accord, or did others say it to you about me?"

Pilate answered,

"Am I a Jew? Your own nation and the chief priests have delivered you over to me. What have you done?"

Jesus answered,

"My kingdom is not of this world. If my kingdom were of this world, my servants would have been fighting, that I might not be delivered over to the Jews. But my kingdom is not from the world."

Then Pilate said to him,

"So you are a king?"

Jesus answered,

"You say that I am a king. For this purpose I was born and for this purpose I have come into the world—to bear witness to the truth. Everyone who is of the truth listens to my voice."

Pilate said to him,

"What is truth?"

After he had said this, he went back outside to the Jews and told them,

"I find no guilt in him."

COMMENTARY

Despite the fact that the Sanhedrin had sentenced Jesus to death, it did not have the legal authority to actually execute Jesus. In order to maintain control, the Romans had reserved the right to mete out capital punishment. For this reason, as soon as the Sanhedrin had produced a formal sentence, they brought Jesus bound to Pilate. Pilate had been appointed as the governor of Judea by Emperor Tiberius (ruled AD 14–37) and served in this capacity from AD 26–36.[38] Normally, Pilate would have been at Caesarea, but during major festivals such as the Passover he came to Jerusalem in order to keep the peace during that politically turbulent time.

John alone provides the initial details of the first phase of the Roman trial.[39] The Jewish leaders do not want to enter the governor's headquarters because it would make them unclean and unable to participate in the ongoing celebrations during the Feast of

---

[38] Jesus was crucified in either AD 30 or 33 (the latter being more likely). If the latter, Pilate's standing with Tiberius had grown more tenuous because Pilate's patron, a man by the name of Sejanus (commander of the praetorian guard in Rome) to whom Pilate likely owed his appointment, had been executed in the interim (on October 18, AD 31, to be exact) on account of treason. This would have rendered Pilate even more vulnerable to pressure by the Jewish leadership (see esp. John 19:12: "If you release this man, you are not Caesar's friend," on which see further below).
[39] John 18:28–32.

Unleavened Bread of which the Passover in a more narrow sense was a part (Luke 22:1). Jews were permitted to enter a Gentile courtyard as long as there was no roof but were considered defiled if they entered a covered Gentile building. Pilate is sensitive to these Jewish concerns and goes out to speak with the Jewish delegation and ask what charges they are bringing against Jesus. The Jewish leaders are initially vague concerning the charges, but when Pilate instructs them to handle the case themselves, they indicate that they cannot do so because Jesus is guilty of the death penalty.[40] John notes that execution by the Romans would fulfill Jesus's prophecy regarding his own death (John 12:33). First-century Jews were horrified by crucifixion and viewed it as equivalent to hanging on a tree—a death indicating that the individual was cursed by God (Deut. 21:23; Gal. 3:13).

The Jewish leaders know that Pilate cares little for the theological charges of blasphemy that mean so much to them, so they emphasize political charges. They claim that Jesus had misled the nation, had forbidden paying tribute to the emperor, and had proclaimed himself to be the messianic king.[41] The charge of blasphemy would not result in Roman execution, but for Jesus to claim kingship meant that he had set himself directly against Caesar as a rival emperor. That was a charge that could stick and, if found to be true, would certainly result in execution.

Pilate responds to these charges by asking Jesus directly: "Are you the King of the Jews?"[42] Pilate only cares about determining whether Jesus is a threat to Roman imperial power. John alone records the brief conversation that ensued. In short, Jesus assures Pilate that he is not a threat to Roman imperial rule in the way that the Jewish leaders have made him out to be: "My kingdom is not of this world. If my kingdom were of this world, my servants would have been fighting, that I might not be delivered over to the Jews. But my kingdom is not from the world." Jesus makes clear that he has no intentions of leading an armed revolt against Roman rule,

---

[40] John 18:31.
[41] Luke 23:2. According to Luke 20:20–26, the second charge was patently false.
[42] Matthew 27:11; Mark 15:2; Luke 23:3; John 18:33.

but his answer prompts Pilate to repeat his initial question: "So you are a king?"[43] Jesus responds with an expression he had used often over the past day: "You have said so."[44] This phrase constitutes a somewhat veiled affirmative, which puts the responsibility back on the questioner.

Jesus proceeds to describe the reason he came into the world: to bear witness to the truth.[45] His kingdom is thus comprised of all who listen to his voice and are open to the truth. Pilate derisively responds: "What is truth?" (a statement laden with irony in light of the fact that the divine embodiment of truth was standing right in front of him).[46] Pilate makes a quick assessment of Jesus based upon his demeanor, appearance, attitude, and answers and concludes that he is not guilty of the charges brought against him, apparently surmising Jesus is a harmless religious teacher and hardly a threat to Roman rule.[47] As the surviving historical records make abundantly clear, Pilate was not accustomed to slavishly complying with the wishes of his subjects, including the Jewish authorities.

The chief priests, however, pounce on Jesus's answer to the kingship question ("You have said so") with an onslaught of intensified accusations. Pilate is greatly amazed when Jesus refuses to answer his accusers. Any other man in Jesus's position would be eager to answer his accusers in the hope of saving his life. But Jesus feared something more than death and had higher priorities than the preservation of life. So he answered not a word in fulfillment of Isaiah 53:7: "He was oppressed, and he was afflicted, yet he opened not his mouth; like a lamb that is led to the slaughter, and like a sheep that before its shearers is silent, so he opened not his mouth." In amazement Pilate asks, "Do you not hear how many things they testify against you?"[48]

Pilate is not sure what to do with Jesus. He thinks Jesus is in-

---

[43] John 18:37.
[44] Matthew 27:11; Mark 15:2; Luke 23:3. See the earlier use of this expression in Matthew 26:25, 64. John indicates the same answer: "You say that I am a king" (John 18:37).
[45] John 18:37.
[46] John 18:38a. See Jesus's earlier statement: "I am the way, and the truth, and the life. No one comes to the Father except through me" (John 14:6).
[47] Luke 23:4; John 18:38.
[48] Matthew 27:13.

nocent, but the Jewish leaders are in a serious uproar. In his amazement and uncertainty, he sees an opening in one of the accusations that might provide a way out and relieve him of having to make a decision. The chief priests and the accompanying crowd of followers had insisted that Jesus was fomenting revolt among the people from Galilee to Judea.[49] Upon inquiring further, Pilate learns that Jesus is indeed a Galilean and therefore under Herod Antipas's jurisdiction.[50] Hoping that Herod would resolve the problem, Pilate sends Jesus and the chief priests over to him.[51] Let Herod deal with Jesus.

From Pontius Pilate to Herod Antipas

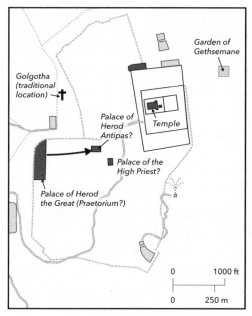

---

[49] Luke 23:5.

[50] Herod Antipas, tetrarch (lit., ruler of one-fourth) of Galilee (4 BC–AD 39), was one of Herod the Great's sons. He had John the Baptist beheaded when the latter denounced Herod's marriage to Herodias (Mark 6:14–29). Jesus referred to Antipas as "that fox" (Luke 13:32).

[51] The Hasmonean palace in Jerusalem, where Herod was probably located, was about a ten-minute walk eastward from Pilate's headquarters.

THE ROMAN TRIAL OF JESUS (PHASE 2): HEROD ANTIPAS

Herod Antipas questions Jesus and sends him back to Pontius Pilate.

LUKE 23:8-12

When Herod saw Jesus, he was very glad, for he had long desired to see him, because he had heard about him, and he was hoping to see some sign done by him.

So he questioned him at some length, but he made no answer.

The chief priests and the scribes stood by, vehemently accusing him.

And Herod with his soldiers treated him with contempt and mocked him.

Then, arraying him in splendid clothing, he sent him back to Pilate.

And Herod and Pilate became friends with each other that very day, for before this they had been at enmity with each other.

COMMENTARY

Luke alone records the details of Jesus's impromptu trial before Herod. Unlike Pilate, Herod had heard of Jesus's miraculous activities throughout Galilee and had long desired to see him in order to personally witness some of those powerful feats. He is delighted that he finally has an opportunity to see a supernatural sign. Herod's delight does not last long—Jesus refuses even to answer any of his questions.

As with Pilate, the chief priests and scribes stand nearby, vehemently accusing Jesus, likely with the same political accusations they had earlier leveled against him. Once Herod realizes that Jesus will not perform a miraculous sign and will not even award him the respect of answering his questions, he and his soldiers begin to mock Jesus and treat him with contempt. Since Jesus is not willing to lower himself and perform for the pleasure of his audience, he becomes the object of sustained verbal abuse. Further abuse consists in Jesus being dressed in fancy royal clothes mocking his claim to be a king, as was customary with political pretenders.

Herod is more interested in seeing a miracle than in determining the truth regarding the Jewish leaders' accusations against Jesus or in solving Pilate's problem. When Jesus refuses to do his bidding, Herod sends him back to Pilate. Luke closes the account with the curious fact that Herod and Pilate became friends that day despite having previously been enemies. A common enemy makes strange bedfellows. Nevertheless, both conclude that Jesus is innocent of the charges that had been brought against him (Luke 23:15).

From Herod Antipas to Pontius Pilate

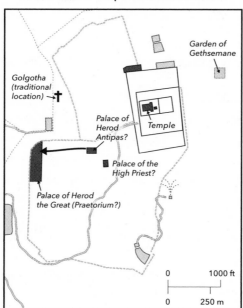

THE ROMAN TRIAL OF JESUS (PHASE 3): THE FINAL VERDICT
Jesus appears before Pilate a second time and is condemned to die.

MATTHEW 27:15-26

Now at the feast the governor was accustomed to release for the crowd any one prisoner whom they wanted. And they had then a notorious prisoner called Barabbas. So when they had gathered, Pilate said to them,

> "Whom do you want me to release for you: Barabbas, or Jesus who is called Christ?"

For he knew that it was out of envy that they had delivered him up. Besides, while he was sitting on the judgment seat, his wife sent word to him,

> "Have nothing to do with that righteous man, for I have suffered much because of him today in a dream."

Now the chief priests and the elders persuaded the crowd to ask for Barabbas and destroy Jesus.

The governor again said to them,

> "Which of the two do you want me to release for you?"

And they said,

> "Barabbas."

Pilate said to them,

> "Then what shall I do with Jesus who is called Christ?"

They all said,

> "Let him be crucified!"

And he said,

> "Why, what evil has he done?"

But they shouted all the more,

> "Let him be crucified!"

So when Pilate saw that he was gaining nothing, but rather that a riot was beginning, he took water and washed his hands before the crowd, saying,

"I am innocent of this man's blood; see to it yourselves."

And all the people answered,

"His blood be on us and on our children!"

Then he released for them Barabbas, and having scourged Jesus, delivered him to be crucified.

MARK 15:6-15

Now at the feast he used to release for them one prisoner for whom they asked. And among the rebels in prison, who had committed murder in the insurrection, there was a man called Barabbas. And the crowd came up and began to ask Pilate to do as he usually did for them. And he answered them, saying,

"Do you want me to release for you the King of the Jews?"

For he perceived that it was out of envy that the chief priests had delivered him up.

But the chief priests stirred up the crowd to have him release for them Barabbas instead.

And Pilate again said to them,

"Then what shall I do with the man you call the King of the Jews?"

And they cried out again,

"Crucify him."

And Pilate said to them,

"Why, what evil has he done?"

But they shouted all the more,

"Crucify him."

So Pilate, wishing to satisfy the crowd, released for them Barabbas, and having scourged Jesus, he delivered him to be crucified.

LUKE 23:13-25

Pilate then called together the chief priests and the rulers and the people, and said to them,

> "You brought me this man as one who was misleading the people.
>
> And after examining him before you, behold, I did not find this man guilty of any of your charges against him.
>
> Neither did Herod, for he sent him back to us.
>
> Look, nothing deserving death has been done by him.
>
> I will therefore punish and release him."

But they all cried out together,

> "Away with this man, and release to us Barabbas"—

a man who had been thrown into prison for an insurrection started in the city and for murder.

Pilate addressed them once more, desiring to release Jesus, but they kept shouting,

> "Crucify, crucify him!"

A third time he said to them,

> "Why, what evil has he done?
>
> I have found in him no guilt deserving death.
>
> I will therefore punish and release him."

But they were urgent, demanding with loud cries that he should be crucified. And their voices prevailed.

So Pilate decided that their demand should be granted.

He released the man who had been thrown into prison for insurrection and murder, for whom they asked, but he delivered Jesus over to their will.

JOHN 18:38b–19:16

After he had said this, he went back outside to the Jews and told them,

> "I find no guilt in him.
>
> But you have a custom that I should release one man for you at the Passover.
>
> So do you want me to release to you the King of the Jews?"

They cried out again,

> "Not this man, but Barabbas!"

Now Barabbas was a robber.

Then Pilate took Jesus and flogged him.

And the soldiers twisted together a crown of thorns and put it on his head and arrayed him in a purple robe.

They came up to him, saying,

> "Hail, King of the Jews!"

and struck him with their hands.

Pilate went out again and said to them,

> "See, I am bringing him out to you that you may know that I find no guilt in him."

So Jesus came out, wearing the crown of thorns and the purple robe.

Pilate said to them,

> "Behold the man!"

When the chief priests and the officers saw him, they cried out,

> "Crucify him, crucify him!"

Pilate said to them,

> "Take him yourselves and crucify him, for I find no guilt in him."

The Jews answered him,

> "We have a law, and according to that law he ought to die because he has made himself the Son of God."

When Pilate heard this statement, he was even more afraid.

He entered his headquarters again and said to Jesus,

> "Where are you from?"

But Jesus gave him no answer.

So Pilate said to him,

> "You will not speak to me?

> Do you not know that I have authority to release you and authority to crucify you?"

Jesus answered him,

> "You would have no authority over me at all unless it had been given you from above.

> Therefore he who delivered me over to you has the greater sin."

From then on Pilate sought to release him, but the Jews cried out,

> "If you release this man, you are not Caesar's friend. Everyone who makes himself a king opposes Caesar."

So when Pilate heard these words, he brought Jesus out and sat down on the judgment seat at a place called The Stone Pavement, and in Aramaic Gabbatha.

Now it was the day of Preparation of the Passover. It was about the sixth hour.

He said to the Jews,

"Behold your King!"

They cried out,

"Away with him, away with him, crucify him!"

Pilate said to them,

"Shall I crucify your King?"

The chief priests answered,

"We have no king but Caesar."

So he delivered him over to them to be crucified.

COMMENTARY

Pilate's Initial Verdict: Not Guilty

When Jesus returns to Pilate from his audience with Herod, Pilate meets with the chief priests and Jewish leaders and renders his verdict: he will punish and release Jesus. Pilate makes clear that both he and Herod found Jesus innocent of the charges that had been brought against him. In their opinion, Jesus did not represent a threat to Roman rule: "Look, nothing deserving death has been done by him" (Luke 23:15), or, as John records the verdict, "I find no guilt in him" (John 18:38). This is how Pilate floats his plan to punish and then release Jesus. Yet his proposal does not satisfy the Jewish leaders.[52]

Barabbas

Still not yielding to the inevitable, Pilate, believing Jesus to be innocent and desiring to see him freed, proposes a solution that he believes will take care of the problem. Apparently, a custom had developed according to which the Roman governor released a prisoner each Passover.[53] Pilate had likely perpetrated this tradition as a way of easing the political tension and anti-Roman sentiment that could have escalated at a time when a large number of pilgrims

---

[52] Luke 23:16–18.
[53] Matthew 27:15; Mark 15:6; Luke 23:18; John 18:39.

gathered in Jerusalem to celebrate God's past deliverance of the Jews from an oppressive foreign regime (i.e., Egypt). Pilate clearly assumes that the crowd will choose Jesus over Barabbas, a violent man who had been imprisoned for taking part in an insurrection and committing robbery and murder.[54]

Pilate does not want Jesus to be executed, because he senses that the Jewish leaders are acting out of mere envy due to Jesus's increasing popularity. At the same time, he does not fully understand, or care about, the theological charges the Jewish authorities are leveling against Jesus.[55] In addition, Matthew records that while Pilate is waiting for an answer from the crowds, his wife sends him an urgent message imploring Pilate to have nothing to do with "that righteous man" (Jesus) because she had suffered a great deal in a dream because of him.[56] Matthew does not provide any additional details, but it is a matter of record that Romans placed a great deal of weight on dreams, visions, and omens. Whatever the specifics of the dream, Pilate's wife connected its message to Jesus and was sufficiently disturbed by it to warn her husband.

The Call for Crucifixion

To Pilate's chagrin, however, the Jewish leaders incite the crowd to ask for the release of Barabbas rather than Jesus.[57] At first, it may seem strange that the people, who earlier in the week had given Jesus a hero's welcome at the Triumphal Entry, would now turn against him, but the activity of the Jewish leaders explains the shift.[58] They are actively stirring up the crowd, no doubt spreading rumors and false accusations, particularly the charge that Jesus had committed blasphemy. Even those in the crowd who were inclined to trust Jesus over against the Jewish leaders would be quite reluctant to support a man guilty of blasphemy. Once the Jewish leaders

---

[54] Mark 15:7; Luke 23:18–19; John 18:40. Note the possible wordplay and irony here: Bar-abbas means "son of the father," while the people reject Jesus, who truly was the "Son of the Father," that is, the divine Son of God.

[55] Matthew 27:18; Mark 15:10.

[56] Matthew 27:19.

[57] Matthew 27:20; Mark 15:11; Luke 23:18; John 18:40.

[58] Alternatively, the "Hosanna!" crowd welcoming him was comprised of Galilean pilgrims and the larger group of disciples, whereas the "Crucify him!" crowd was Jerusalemites.

got the ball rolling in inciting the crowd, it became an easy task to maintain the mob mentality and fury.

Despite the crowd's choice of Barabbas, Pilate attempts to carry out his earlier stated intention to punish and release Jesus. He has Jesus flogged, during which time the soldiers mock Jesus by placing a crown of thorns on his head and a purple robe on his tattered body. They pretend to offer him respect and honor as a king and then strike him with their hands.[59] Ironically, the soldiers mock the true king of the entire universe! This initial pre-sentence flogging would have been much lighter than the post-sentence scourging that Jesus will later endure.[60] After having Jesus flogged, Pilate presents him to the crowd in order to demonstrate that he did not think Jesus deserved death—he had administered the punishment that he thought Jesus deserved.[61] At this point, Matthew and Mark record Pilate as asking, "Then what shall I do with the man you call the King of the Jews?"[62] This question leads to what are among the most famous and chilling words in the Gospels: "Crucify him."[63]

Pilate is not ready to acquiesce to the Jewish authorities' demands yet and sarcastically refuses to comply, instructing them to crucify Jesus themselves, something he knows they cannot legally do.[64] The Jewish leaders, sensing that victory is imminent, ignore Pilate's refusal and continue to insist that according to their law, Jesus must die because he had "made himself the Son of God."[65] This statement frightens Pilate. He is not scared of the Jews but of the possible divine origin of Jesus—which would explain his wife's fearful dream. Speaking alone with Jesus, he asks, "Where are you from?"[66] When Jesus refuses to respond, Pilate issues a

---

[59] John 19:1–3.

[60] Some interpreters view the two accounts of flogging as identical, but it is not likely that Pilate would have ordered such a severe punishment for someone who was not yet convicted. The initial flogging recorded in John 19:1–3 and Luke 23:16 likely corresponds to the *fustigatio*, the lighter form of flogging reserved for minor crimes, while the later scourging recorded in Matthew 27:26 and Mark 15:15 in all probability points to the *verberatio*, a severe beating associated with capital punishment.

[61] John 19:4–5.

[62] Mark 15:12. Matthew 27:22 similarly records Pilate's question: "Then what shall I do with Jesus who is called Christ?"

[63] Matthew 27:22; Mark 15:13; Luke 23:21.

[64] John 19:6.

[65] John 19:7.

[66] John 19:9.

veiled threat: "You will not speak to me? Do you not know that I have authority to release you and authority to crucify you?"[67]

Jesus promptly puts Pilate in his place by answering, "You would have no authority over me at all unless it had been given you from above."[68] It was humanly absurd for an accused man to respond in such a way. Who did Jesus think he was? Pilate, the Jewish leaders, and the crowds are in turmoil, but Jesus calmly expresses faith in God. He is not afraid, for he knows that no human authority will decide his fate.

Pilate leaves that brief encounter with a renewed desire to release Jesus, but the Jewish leaders intensify their efforts and begin to apply serious political pressure: "If you release this man, you are not Caesar's friend. Everyone who makes himself a king opposes Caesar."[69] With this statement, the Jewish leaders are effectively threatening Pilate. If he lets Jesus go, news will find its way back to Rome that Pilate is not watching out for Caesar's interests by disposing of rival kings. Such an accusation could endanger Pilate's political ambitions if not his very survival as governor.

"Crucify him!" The crowd screams out those words again and again. Pilate tries to intervene by reasoning with the crowd, "Why, what evil has he done?"[70] But the crowd ignores Pilate and drowns him out with their repeated cries for Jesus's crucifixion. "Shall I crucify your King?" Pilate asks, to which the Jews shockingly reply, "We have no king but Caesar."[71] In their abject blindness and desire to get rid of Jesus, the Jewish leaders deny their national heritage, according to which God alone is king (Judg. 8:23; 1 Sam. 8:7), as well as their messianic expectations.

The Final Verdict

The situation seemed to be rapidly spinning out of control. All the ingredients for a perfect storm were in place—a storm of riot,

---

[67] John 19:10.
[68] John 19:11.
[69] John 19:12.
[70] Matthew 27:23; Mark 15:14; Luke 23:22. Pilate's repeated insistence upon Jesus's innocence confirms Old Testament prophetic predictions in Psalm 38:20–21 and Isaiah 53:9.
[71] John 19:15–16.

cruel Roman oppression, and bloodshed. Pilate renders his final decision on the basis of practical expediency rather than truth and justice. He firmly believes Jesus to be innocent but fears a riot and desires to satisfy the crowd.[72] Mob justice is an oxymoron, since the whim of a mob rarely (if ever) leads to genuine justice. Pilate had good reason to fear a riot—the Jewish people were prone to civil disturbances throughout the first century, and one of his main jobs as governor was to keep the peace at whatever cost. Surely the death of one innocent man was worth avoiding the greater bloodshed sure to follow a riot.

Before communicating his final decision, Pilate engages in a symbolic action—he washes his hands in front of the entire crowd in order to indicate that he was innocent of Jesus's blood.[73] The crowds respond to Pilate's action by accepting responsibility for Jesus's death: "His blood be on us and on our children!"[74] Despite all of Pilate's efforts to exonerate himself and to profess his innocence regarding Jesus's death, the fact remains that he was responsible—the whole terrible affair occurred under his jurisdiction and oversight. No matter how much Pilate tried to assert his neutrality in the matter, he could not render the Jewish leaders solely responsible for Jesus's death.

The final stage of Jesus's Roman trial concludes with a scourging.[75] Roman scourging was so brutal and violent that prisoners would occasionally die before the crucifixion. Even though Jesus survives this form of torture, the beating ensures he will die before sundown. During the scourging, he is tied to a post and beaten with a whip interwoven with bone and metal until his skin and tissue are shredded. The irony in each Gospel account is palpable: Jesus, a righteous man, is condemned to death while Barabbas, a guilty man, goes free. Jesus, a man declared not guilty by the Roman governor, is nonetheless given over for execution—an outrageous and transparent miscarriage of justice. John notes that this final verdict came about at the sixth hour (approaching noon) on

---

[72] Matthew 27:24; Mark 15:15; Luke 23:23–24.
[73] Matthew 27:24.
[74] Matthew 27:25.
[75] Matthew 27:26; Mark 15:15.

the day of Preparation of the Passover, the time that lambs would be slain for the Sabbath dinner of Passover week. This connection further emphasizes that Jesus was the Lamb of God who would take away the sin of the world.[76]

Jewish Reckoning of Time

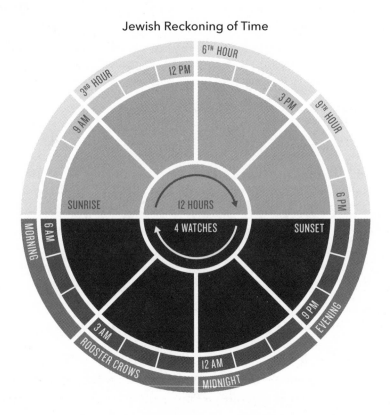

First-century Jews thought of a day as the twelve hours from dawn until dusk (John 11:9). The crucifixion accounts mention only three time designations: the third hour, the sixth hour, and the ninth hour, which suggests that the day was considered to fall roughly into four quarters. Similarly, dusk until dawn was divided into four watches of the night: the evening, midnight, when the rooster crows, and the morning (Mark 13:35).

---

[76] See John 1:29. This should not be seen as a contradiction of Mark, who notes that the crucifixion took place around the third hour (Mark 15:25). Both John and Mark were giving an approximate time (note John's use of "about"). What is more, ancient people did not keep precise time.

We should remember that sundials were rarely used in the first century and that the times of sunrise and sunset change as the seasons change. Time designations were very general and based upon the sun's position in the sky. The "third hour" of Mark 15:25 is probably not a precise reference to 9 a.m. but rather a general reference to the quarter of a day surrounding 9 a.m., that is, anytime between approximately 7:30 or 8:00 a.m. and 10:00 or 10:30 a.m.

Likewise, "sixth hour" could refer to any time from between around 10:30 or 11:00 a.m. to 1:00 or 1:30 p.m. If the sentencing was delivered, say, around 10:30 a.m., and two witnesses were to glance at the sun in the sky, one could round down to the "third hour" while the other might round up to "about the sixth hour," depending also on other factors they might want to emphasize.

———•◦•———

THE ROAD TO GOLGOTHA
Jesus is mocked and marched to Golgotha.

MATTHEW 27:27-34

Then the soldiers of the governor took Jesus into the governor's headquarters, and they gathered the whole battalion before him.

And they stripped him and put a scarlet robe on him, and twisting together a crown of thorns, they put it on his head and put a reed in his right hand.

And kneeling before him, they mocked him, saying,

"Hail, King of the Jews!"

And they spit on him and took the reed and struck him on the head.

And when they had mocked him, they stripped him of the robe and put his own clothes on him and led him away to crucify him.

As they went out, they found a man of Cyrene, Simon by name. They compelled this man to carry his cross.

And when they came to a place called Golgotha (which means Place of a Skull), they offered him wine to drink, mixed with gall, but when he tasted it, he would not drink it.

MARK 15:16-23

And the soldiers led him away inside the palace (that is, the governor's headquarters), and they called together the whole battalion.

And they clothed him in a purple cloak, and twisting together a crown of thorns, they put it on him.

And they began to salute him,

"Hail, King of the Jews!"

And they were striking his head with a reed and spitting on him and kneeling down in homage to him.

And when they had mocked him, they stripped him of the purple cloak and put his own clothes on him.

And they led him out to crucify him.

And they compelled a passerby, Simon of Cyrene, who was coming in from the country, the father of Alexander and Rufus, to carry his cross. And they brought him to the place called Golgotha (which means Place of a Skull). And they offered him wine mixed with myrrh, but he did not take it.

LUKE 23:26-31

And as they led him away, they seized one Simon of Cyrene, who was coming in from the country, and laid on him the cross, to carry it behind Jesus.

And there followed him a great multitude of the people and of women who were mourning and lamenting for him.

But turning to them Jesus said,

"Daughters of Jerusalem, do not weep for me, but weep for yourselves and for your children. For behold, the days are coming when they will say,

'Blessed are the barren and the wombs that never bore and the breasts that never nursed!'

Then they will begin to say to the mountains,

'Fall on us,'

and to the hills,

'Cover us.'

For if they do these things when the wood is green, what will happen when it is dry?"

JOHN 19:16b-17

So they took Jesus, and he went out, bearing his own cross, to the place called The Place of a Skull, which in Aramaic is called Golgotha.

From Pontius Pilate to Golgotha

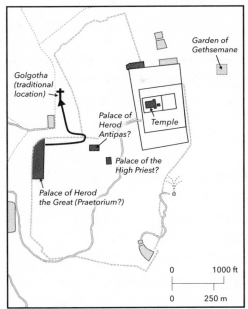

COMMENTARY

Following Pilate's verdict, an entire battalion of Roman soldiers—around six hundred men—gather to mock Jesus in the governor's headquarters, the praetorium, which also served as a fortress.[77] Roman soldiers in Jerusalem were known to play cruel games with condemned prisoners, so their actions in regard to Jesus are not out of character. They dress him up as a pretend emperor with a violet-red robe, a crown of thorns, and a reed for a scepter, and pretend to honor him by kneeling and acclaiming his kingship: "Hail, King of the Jews!"[78] They proceed to further degrade him by spitting on him and striking him on his thorn-crowned head with his scepter, the reed.

It is possible that the mockery recorded by Matthew and Mark is the same as that recorded by John, since both instances reference a crown of thorns, acclamations of kingship, and the use of a royal purple robe to intensify the mockery.[79] If these depictions do describe the same event, the different order (pre-verdict in John and post-verdict in Matthew and Mark) only indicates different narrative arrangements, since the events took place so closely in time. It is quite possible, however, that the events are distinct—the mockery of Christ's kingship had become a running joke among his captors from the temple guards at his Jewish trial,[80] Herod and his soldiers (Luke 23:11), and the guards who administered his initial flogging (John 19:1–3). Jesus's captors couldn't seem to get enough laughter at his expense—oblivious to the reality of his true kingship. When they grow tired of mocking Jesus, the soldiers lead him away to be crucified.

Jesus begins the journey to Golgotha carrying his cross—passing through the Gennath (Garden) Gate and outside the western second wall of Jerusalem—but at some point along the way the

---

[77] The reference to the entire battalion may also refer to a maniple, a subdivision of 120 to 200 soldiers.

[78] Matthew 27:29. Matthew records the robe as being scarlet while Mark and John describe the robe as purple, but, as it is today, borderline colors may be described differently by different people without representing a contradiction.

[79] Mark 15:16–20; John 19:1–3. See the earlier scene in front of Herod Antipas.

[80] Matthew 26:67–68; Mark 14:65; Luke 22:63–65.

Roman soldiers force a man named Simon from Cyrene to carry Jesus's cross (likely weighing 30 to 40 pounds) because Jesus is too weak from loss of blood to continue carrying it.[81] Cyrene, a region of North Africa, had a large Jewish population, and Simon was likely a Jewish Passover pilgrim. Mark's mention of Simon's sons Alexander and Rufus may be because Rufus later became an active member of one of the Roman house churches (Rom. 16:13) and was personally known to Mark and the readers of his Gospel.[82]

Luke alone records Jesus's final dire prophecy. Jesus hears the mourning and lamenting of some women in the crowd that throng around his execution processional. Gathering his strength, he turns to them and, using the language of Zechariah 12:10–14 and Hosea 10:8, prophesies that terrible days lie ahead for Jerusalem: "Daughters of Jerusalem, do not weep for me, but weep for yourselves and for your children. For behold, the days are coming when they will say, 'Blessed are the barren and the wombs that never bore and the breasts that never nursed!'"[83] Jesus is predicting the terror and calamity that will befall Jerusalem when it will be destroyed by the Romans in AD 70—within a generation, the entire nation will be decimated! Josephus, a first-century Jewish historian who personally lived through those grim events, records how thousands of Jews were crucified by the Romans during those dark days.

When they arrive at Golgotha, the soldiers offer Jesus wine mixed with gall and myrrh, possibly as a mild sedative or another form of mockery because of its bitter taste.[84] Regardless of the reason it was offered, after tasting it Jesus refuses the drink. It is not clear how Golgotha acquired its name, which meant "Place of the Skull." It could be because the place was a popular location for Roman executions, or because there were many tombs in the local vicinity, or because the geography itself, perhaps on a low cliff or hill, resembled a human skull. Regardless of the reason for

---

[81] Matthew 27:32; Mark 15:21; Luke 23:26; John 19:17.
[82] Mark 15:21.
[83] Luke 23:28–29.
[84] Matthew 27:34; Mark 15:23; Luke 23:36.

its name, the site of Jesus's crucifixion was a location outside the city in keeping with Old Testament requirements for executions.[85]

◆•◆•◆

THE CRUCIFIXION

Jesus is crucified between two thieves.

MATTHEW 27:35-44

And when they had crucified him, they divided his garments among them by casting lots. Then they sat down and kept watch over him there.

And over his head they put the charge against him, which read,

"This is Jesus, the King of the Jews."

Then two robbers were crucified with him, one on the right and one on the left.

And those who passed by derided him, wagging their heads and saying,

"You who would destroy the temple and rebuild it in three days, save yourself!

If you are the Son of God, come down from the cross."

So also the chief priests, with the scribes and elders, mocked him, saying,

"He saved others; he cannot save himself.

He is the King of Israel; let him come down now from the cross, and we will believe in him.

He trusts in God; let God deliver him now, if he desires him.

For he said, 'I am the Son of God.'"

---

[85] Leviticus 24:14, 23; Numbers 15:35–36; Deuteronomy 17:5; 21:19–21; 22:24; Hebrews 13:12.

And the robbers who were crucified with him also reviled him in the same way.

MARK 15:24-32

And they crucified him and divided his garments among them, casting lots for them, to decide what each should take.

And it was the third hour when they crucified him.

And the inscription of the charge against him read,

"The King of the Jews."

And with him they crucified two robbers, one on his right and one on his left.

And those who passed by derided him, wagging their heads and saying,

"Aha! You who would destroy the temple and rebuild it in three days, save yourself, and come down from the cross!"

So also the chief priests with the scribes mocked him to one another, saying,

"He saved others; he cannot save himself.

Let the Christ, the King of Israel, come down now from the cross that we may see and believe."

Those who were crucified with him also reviled him.

LUKE 23:33-43

And when they came to the place that is called The Skull, there they crucified him, and the criminals, one on his right and one on his left.

And Jesus said,

"Father, forgive them, for they know not what they do."

And they cast lots to divide his garments.

And the people stood by, watching, but the rulers scoffed at him, saying,

> "He saved others; let him save himself, if he is the Christ of God, his Chosen One!"

The soldiers also mocked him, coming up and offering him sour wine and saying,

> "If you are the King of the Jews, save yourself!"

There was also an inscription over him,

> "This is the King of the Jews."

One of the criminals who were hanged railed at him, saying,

> "Are you not the Christ?
>
> Save yourself and us!"

But the other rebuked him, saying,

> "Do you not fear God, since you are under the same sentence of condemnation?
>
> And we indeed justly, for we are receiving the due reward of our deeds; but this man has done nothing wrong."

And he said,

> "Jesus, remember me when you come into your kingdom."

And he said to him,

> "Truly, I say to you, today you will be with me in Paradise."

JOHN 19:18-27

There they crucified him, and with him two others, one on either side, and Jesus between them.

Pilate also wrote an inscription and put it on the cross. It read,

> "Jesus of Nazareth, the King of the Jews."

Many of the Jews read this inscription, for the place where Jesus was crucified was near the city, and it was written in Aramaic, in Latin, and in Greek. So the chief priests of the Jews said to Pilate,

"Do not write,

'The King of the Jews,'

but rather,

'This man said, I am King of the Jews.'"

Pilate answered,

"What I have written I have written."

When the soldiers had crucified Jesus, they took his garments and divided them into four parts, one part for each soldier; also his tunic. But the tunic was seamless, woven in one piece from top to bottom, so they said to one another,

"Let us not tear it, but cast lots for it to see whose it shall be."

This was to fulfill the Scripture which says,

"They divided my garments among them,
and for my clothing they cast lots." [Ps. 22:18]

So the soldiers did these things, but standing by the cross of Jesus were his mother and his mother's sister, Mary the wife of Clopas, and Mary Magdalene.

When Jesus saw his mother and the disciple whom he loved standing nearby, he said to his mother,

"Woman, behold, your son!"

Then he said to the disciple,

"Behold, your mother!"

And from that hour the disciple took her to his own home.

COMMENTARY

None of the Gospel authors provides any details concerning the actual crucifixion; each simply notes the fact that the soldiers crucified Jesus.[86] Most first-century readers would have had some idea of the physical torture and public shame that crucifixion involved. Victims either died from physical trauma, loss of blood, or shock or succumbed to suffocation when they no longer had the strength to lift themselves up to breathe. The Romans employed a number of different crucifixion techniques, but the use of nails and a crossbar was common.

Jesus's enemies continue to mock him to the very end. Those passing by—and there would have been many pilgrims passing by to take part in the ongoing festival—deride and taunt him: "If you are the Son of God, come down from the cross."[87] The Jewish leaders do not pass up the opportunity to publicly humiliate the one who had opposed their hypocrisy: "He saved others; he cannot save himself. He is the King of Israel; let him come down now from the cross, and we will believe in him. He trusts in God; let God deliver him now, if he desires him. For he said, 'I am the Son of God.'"[88] Jesus's suffering and impending death on the cross seem to validate the charges of the Jewish leaders; from all appearances, God was punishing Jesus for his blasphemy. The false offer of the Jewish leaders to believe if Jesus supernaturally came down from the cross likely elicited some laughter, but Jesus's enemies would not get the last laugh. There is deep irony in the fact that if Jesus had come down from the cross he would have saved himself but not others.

Luke records that Jesus responds to the crucifixion and the mockery with the powerfully haunting words, "Father, forgive them, for they know not what they do."[89] These compelling, convicting words communicate God's indescribable love for his creation. Even in the midst of torture and mockery, Jesus extends forgiveness to his tormentors and embodies his earlier teaching

---

[86] Matthew 27:35a; Mark 15:24a; Luke 23:23; John 19:18.
[87] Matthew 27:39–40. See also Mark 15:29–30.
[88] Matthew 27:42–43. See also Mark 15:31–32; Luke 23:35.
[89] Luke 23:34.

on loving one's enemies (Matt. 5:43–48; Luke 6:27–36). Jesus's words also foreshadow the forgiveness through faith in him that would soon be proclaimed throughout the entire known world, fulfilling the words of Isaiah 53:12 ("Yet he bore the sin of many, and makes intercession for the transgressors") and serving as a model for Christians to emulate as they have faced persecution and martyrdom throughout the centuries.[90]

John records that several of Jesus's followers—his mother, Mary; the beloved disciple (likely John the apostle); and a few other women—stand near the cross at some point during the crucifixion.[91] Despite Jesus's suffering, he makes sure to look after his mother, since his adoptive father Joseph had apparently already died and she would have had little to no personal income. Jesus entrusts Mary to the beloved disciple (perhaps because her other sons were not yet believers; John 7:5; see also Matt. 13:57; Mark 3:21, 31; 6:4) and charges him to take care of her ("Behold, your mother!").[92] John notes that from that time, that disciple took Mary into his own home.[93]

The Two Robbers

Each Gospel notes that Jesus is not crucified alone but is executed along with two robbers, one on either side.[94] This fulfilled Isaiah's prophecy that the suffering servant would be "numbered with the transgressors" (Isa. 53:12). Both robbers initially join in the mockery and revile Jesus along with the others.[95]

Luke alone records how one of the robbers experiences a change of heart, perhaps after hearing Jesus pray that God might forgive those responsible for his crucifixion. This robber rebukes the other and notes that while they are suffering the just penalty

---

[90] Acts 7:60; 1 Peter 2:21–24.

[91] John 19:25–26. See further the discussion of the Synoptic references to the women at the cross in the next section below.

[92] John 19:27. Mary's other sons were named James (author of the epistle of James), Joseph/Joses, Simon, and Judas/Jude (author of the epistle of Jude) (Matt. 13:55; Mark 6:2–3; Acts 1:14; 1 Cor. 9:4–5; Gal. 1:19). She also had at least two daughters (Mark 6:3).

[93] John 19:27.

[94] Matthew 27:38; Mark 15:27; Luke 23:32–33; John 19:18.

[95] Matthew 27:44; Mark 15:32.

for their crimes, Jesus is suffering as an innocent man (thus revealing faith in Jesus). The repentant robber then turns to Jesus and entreats him: "Jesus, remember me when you come into your kingdom,"[96] to which Jesus responds, "Truly, I say to you, today you will be with me in Paradise."[97] Jesus's acceptance of the man powerfully illustrates the opportunity for forgiveness and eternal life that will soon be proclaimed to all people on the basis of his sacrificial death for sin. The robber has no time or ability to do any good works—he could not possibly make up for the wrong he had done if that were even possible—but he does have the strength to believe in Jesus and ask him for salvation. That is all that is needed, and the man's eternal destiny changes decisively from separation from God to spending eternity with Jesus in Paradise.

The Charge

Pilate has the charge against Jesus inscribed above his head on the cross. John notes that the inscription read, "Jesus of Nazareth, the King of the Jews."[98] This public notice of a crucified person's crime was intended by the Romans to serve as a deterrent to any other would-be kings. Rome would accept only one emperor. With this charge, Pilate also justifies his actions in allowing an innocent man to be executed. Jesus is officially executed as a political rebel and insurrectionist who claimed to be king of the Jews. John notes that this inscription was written in Aramaic (the common language of Palestine), Latin (the official Roman language), and Greek (the international language of the empire) in order to ensure the widest possible readership among the throngs of Passover pilgrims.[99]

---

[96] Luke 23:42.

[97] Luke 23:43. The thief had only asked Jesus to remember him when he would come into his kingdom (v. 42). Jesus, in reply, tells him that he would be with him in Paradise "today." The Septuagint (Greek translation of the Old Testament) refers to the garden of Eden by using the same Greek word (see also Gen. 2:8–9). Jesus's words may hint at the restoration of the intimate relationship humans enjoyed with God prior to the fall. This restoration occurs instantaneously upon conversion, although it is fully consummated only in the eternal state.

[98] John 19:19. The other Gospel authors abbreviate slightly to focus on the charge itself. Matthew notes that the inscription read, "This is Jesus, the King of the Jews" (Matt. 27:37). Mark sums up the content of the inscription as "The King of the Jews" (Mark 15:26), while Luke glosses it as "This is the King of the Jews" (Luke 23:38). See the chart on p. 20.

[99] John 19:20.

Jesus's Crucifixion Epitaph in Greek, Latin, and Aramaic

ΙΗΣΟΥΣ ΝΑΖΩΡΑΙΟΣ ΒΑΣΙΛΕΥΣ ΤΩΝ ΙΟΥΔΑΙΩΝ

IESVS NAZARENVS REX IVDÆORVM

ישוע נצרתא מלך יהודיא

The chief priests approach Pilate and request that he change the charge to say, "This man *said*, 'I am King of the Jews,'" but Pilate refuses their request. They had already manipulated him to execute Jesus by threatening him and stirring up a riot, and he has no desire to acquiesce to their demands on this point.[100] In truth, of course, as John hints in fine irony, Pilate was executing Jesus for actually being the King of the Jews. This charge, which was the basis for Jesus's condemnation and execution by the Romans, quickly became a confession of truth for the early Christians and believers through the centuries.[101] Jesus was not just a king; he is *the* king, and he will return one day to finally and fully establish God's kingdom on his newly created heaven and earth.

Gambling for Jesus's Clothes

After lifting up Jesus on the cross, the soldiers divide his remaining earthly possessions, that is, the clothes he had been wearing.[102] This probably included his head covering, garments, belt, and sandals. Because Jesus's inner tunic was one seamless piece, the soldiers decide to cast lots for it; it would hardly be worth anything if it were torn up and divided evenly. By this action, the Roman soldiers unwittingly fulfill the psalmist's prophecy: "They divide my garments among them, and for my clothing they cast lots" (Ps. 22:18). It is remarkable that at the end of Jesus's life all of his worldly possessions consisted of the clothes on his back. His was hardly a successful life by natural standards—he left no

---

[100] John 19:21–22.
[101] On crucifixes and representations of the crucifixion in both the Western and Eastern Church, the inscription was usually depicted by acronym: either INRI (Latin: Iēsus Nazarēnus, Rēx Iūdaeōrum) or INBI (Greek: Ἰησοῦς ὁ Ναζωραῖος ὁ βασιλεὺς τῶν Ἰουδαίων).
[102] Matthew 27:35; Mark 15:24; Luke 23:24; John 19:23–24.

descendants, and he had no property or wealth. Yet despite his "failure" to make much of himself by worldly standards, Jesus's life, ministry, message, death, and resurrection literally changed the course of world history and made it possible for human beings to be reconciled to God and experience eternal salvation.

The Last Seven Sayings of Jesus

"Father, forgive them, for they know not what they do."	Luke 23:34
"Truly, I say to you, today you will be with me in Paradise."	Luke 23:43
"Woman, behold, your son! . . . Behold, your mother!"	John 19:26–27
"Eli, Eli, lema sabachthani?" that is, "My God, my God, why have you forsaken me?"	Matt. 27:46; Mark 15:34
"I thirst."	John 19:28
"It is finished."	John 19:30
"Father, into your hands I commit my spirit!"	Luke 23:46

THE DEATH OF JESUS

Jesus breathes his last.

MATTHEW 27:45-56

Now from the sixth hour there was darkness over all the land until the ninth hour.

And about the ninth hour Jesus cried out with a loud voice, saying,

"Eli, Eli, lema sabachthani?"

that is,

"My God, my God, why have you forsaken me?" [Ps. 22:1]

And some of the bystanders, hearing it, said,

"This man is calling Elijah."

And one of them at once ran and took a sponge, filled it with sour wine, and put it on a reed and gave it to him to drink. But the others said,

"Wait, let us see whether Elijah will come to save him."

And Jesus cried out again with a loud voice and yielded up his spirit.

And behold, the curtain of the temple was torn in two, from top to bottom.

And the earth shook, and the rocks were split. The tombs also were opened. And many bodies of the saints who had fallen asleep were raised, and coming out of the tombs after his resurrection they went into the holy city and appeared to many.

When the centurion and those who were with him, keeping watch over Jesus, saw the earthquake and what took place, they were filled with awe and said,

"Truly this was the Son of God!"

There were also many women there, looking on from a distance, who had followed Jesus from Galilee, ministering to him, among whom were Mary Magdalene and Mary the mother of James and Joseph and the mother of the sons of Zebedee.

MARK 15:33-41

And when the sixth hour had come, there was darkness over the whole land until the ninth hour.

And at the ninth hour Jesus cried with a loud voice,

"Eloi, Eloi, lema sabachthani?"

which means,

"My God, my God, why have you forsaken me?" [Ps. 22:1]

And some of the bystanders hearing it said,

"Behold, he is calling Elijah."

And someone ran and filled a sponge with sour wine, put it on a reed and gave it to him to drink, saying,

"Wait, let us see whether Elijah will come to take him down."

And Jesus uttered a loud cry and breathed his last.

And the curtain of the temple was torn in two, from top to bottom.

And when the centurion, who stood facing him, saw that in this way he breathed his last, he said,

"Truly this man was the Son of God!"

There were also women looking on from a distance, among whom were Mary Magdalene, and Mary the mother of James the younger and of Joses, and Salome. When he was in Galilee, they followed him and ministered to him, and there were also many other women who came up with him to Jerusalem.

LUKE 23:44–49

It was now about the sixth hour, and there was darkness over the whole land until the ninth hour, while the sun's light failed.

And the curtain of the temple was torn in two.

Then Jesus, calling out with a loud voice, said,

"Father, into your hands I commit my spirit!"

And having said this he breathed his last.

Now when the centurion saw what had taken place, he praised God, saying,

"Certainly this man was innocent!"

And all the crowds that had assembled for this spectacle, when they saw what had taken place, returned home beating their breasts. And all his acquaintances and the women who had followed him from Galilee stood at a distance watching these things.

JOHN 19:28-37

After this, Jesus, knowing that all was now finished, said (to fulfill the Scripture),

"I thirst."

A jar full of sour wine stood there, so they put a sponge full of the sour wine on a hyssop branch and held it to his mouth. When Jesus had received the sour wine, he said,

"It is finished,"

and he bowed his head and gave up his spirit.

Since it was the day of Preparation, and so that the bodies would not remain on the cross on the Sabbath (for that Sabbath was a high day), the Jews asked Pilate that their legs might be broken and that they might be taken away. So the soldiers came and broke the legs of the first, and of the other who had been crucified with him. But when they came to Jesus and saw that he was already dead, they did not break his legs. But one of the soldiers pierced his side with a spear, and at once there came out blood and water.

He who saw it has borne witness—his testimony is true, and he knows that he is telling the truth—that you also may believe. For these things took place that the Scripture might be fulfilled:

"Not one of his bones will be broken." [Ps. 34:20]

And again another Scripture says,

"They will look on him whom they have pierced." [Zech. 12:10]

COMMENTARY

Darkness Covers the Land

Jesus hangs on the cross for approximately six hours. Mark notes that they crucified Jesus around the third hour (mid-morning) and an unusual darkness covered the land from the sixth hour (around noon) until the ninth hour (mid-afternoon), the brightest and hottest part of the day.[103] This darkness was a supernatural act of God and not a solar eclipse, because a solar eclipse requires a new moon whereas Passover took place during a full moon. In the Old Testament, darkness could represent a situation of human ignorance and sin (Isa. 60:1–3), divine lament (Amos 8:9–10), or divine judgment (Ex. 10:21–23; Amos 5:18, 20; Joel 2:10, 30–31; 3:14–16). Here, it likely communicates all of these senses: Jesus was bearing God's judgment for the sin of the world, yet the tragic death of an innocent man should result in sorrow and lament.

Jesus Dies

At the ninth hour, Jesus utters a despairing cry: "My God, my God, why have you forsaken me?"[104] Jesus drew this lament of utter God-forsakenness from Psalm 22:1, which states, "My God, my God, why have you forsaken me? Why are you so far from saving me, from the words of my groaning?" In some mysterious way beyond our human understanding, Jesus, the second person of the Trinity, is cut off and separated from God because he is bearing the sin of humanity and enduring God's wrath as a substitute for and in place of sinful humans.[105] Of course, Jesus knows how Psalm 22 ends—in vindication—and may be reminding us that forsakenness is not the end of the story.

Jesus's cry does not indicate that he was bewildered or confused—as if he actually expected God to rescue him from the cross and was disappointed—but rather expresses the terrifying cost of

---

103 Matthew 27:45; Mark 15:33; Luke 23:44–45.
104 Matthew 27:46; Mark 15:34.
105 As the apostle Paul put it memorably, "For our sake he [God the Father] made him [Jesus] to be sin who knew no sin, so that in him we might become the righteousness of God" (2 Cor. 5:21).

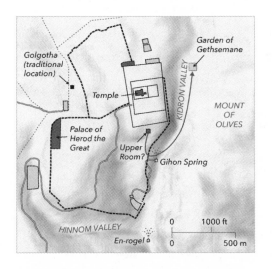

The Last Supper

After Jesus and his disciples ate the Passover meal, they crossed the Kidron Valley and entered a garden called Gethsemane (meaning "oil press"), where they often spent time while visiting Jerusalem (cf. Luke 22:39).

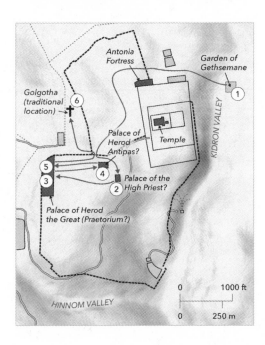

Jesus's Arrest, Trial, and Crucifixion

The path from Jesus's arrest to his crucifixion (part of which is often called the Via Dolorosa, "Way of Sorrows") is difficult to retrace with certainty; the traditional route was fixed by Franciscan monks in the fourteenth century. The Bible records that after the Passover meal, Judas led a contingent of soldiers to Gethsemane to arrest Jesus (1). From there Jesus was led to Annas (location unknown), who sent him to his son-in-law Caiaphas, the high priest (2). The Jewish leaders then appealed to the Roman governor Pilate to have Jesus put to death (3). Luke records that Pilate sent Jesus to Herod Antipas (4), who questioned Jesus but returned him to Pilate without rendering any judgment (5). Pilate then sent Jesus to be crucified at Golgotha (6).

1. The **Gate of the Essenes** allowed the Essenes to access latrines outside the city walls in accordance with their strict laws of hygiene.

2. **Herod's Palace** was the Jerusalem home of Herod the Great from 23 to 4 BC Pilate, who normally resided in Caesarea Maritima, resided in this palace during his visits to Jerusalem, including his visit for the Passover preceding Christ's crucifixion.

3. The **Praetorium** was in Herod's Palace (Matt. 27:27; Mark 15:16), which served as Pilate's official headquarters and as a fortress. A raised stone pavement, used for official judgments, stood outside the palace and was the site of Jesus's condemnation under Pilate (John 19:13).

4. Herod the Great fortified three towers to protect his palace:
5. from west to east there was the **Tower of Hippicus** (155
6. feet/47 m tall), the **Tower of Phasael** (138 feet/42 m tall), and the **Tower of Mariamne** (95 feet/29 m tall).

7. The two-level **Palatial Mansion** (6,500 sq. feet/604 sq. m) may have been the Palace of Annas, who served as high priest from AD 6 to 15. Annas's son-in-law Caiaphas held this

office from AD 18 to 36 and presided at the trial of Jesus (Matt. 26:57).

8. This is often considered the most likely location of **Golgotha,** the place of Jesus's death. It was on a hill overlooking a quarry, outside the Second Wall of the city and near the Gennath (Garden) Gate.

9. Herod the Great lived in the luxurious **Hasmonean Palace** from the mid-30s to 23 BC while awaiting the building of his own new palace. Herod Antipas ("Herod the Tetrarch") lived in this palace during his reign, 4 BC–AD 39. Jesus appeared before him here in either AD 30 or 33.

10. The **Archives** building contained the public registers (including genealogies) as well as bonds taken by moneylenders, which allowed the recovery of debts.

11. The **Xystus,** built on the site of the former Greek Gymnasium, was a place of mass assembly.

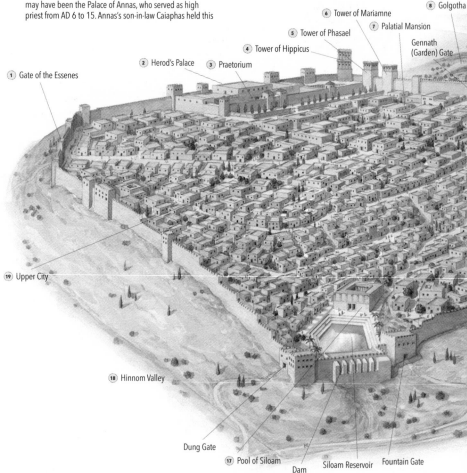

6 Tower of Mariamne

8 Golgotha

7 Palatial Mansion

5 Tower of Phasael

Gennath (Garden) Gate

4 Tower of Hippicus

2 Herod's Palace   3 Praetorium

1 Gate of the Essenes

19 Upper City

18 Hinnom Valley

Dung Gate

17 Pool of Siloam

Dam

Siloam Reservoir

Fountain Gate

⑫ The **Council House** was a public building, perhaps functioning as a municipal office.

⑬ **The Temple** was reconstructed by Herod the Great, beginning in 20/19 BC

⑭ The **Bethesda Pools** (see John 5:2) were twin pools, each measuring c. 312 by 164–196 feet (95 by 50–60 m), and c. 50 feet (15 m) deep. A small Roman temple dedicated to Aesculapius stood to the east of the pools.

⑮ The **Garden of Gethsemane** was located approximately 300 yards (274 m) from Jerusalem and the Temple Mount. The Mount of Olives was "a Sabbath day's journey away" from Jerusalem (Acts 1:12), approximately 1,100 yards, or 3/5 of a mile.

⑯ The ravine of the **Kidron Valley** has always served as Jerusalem's eastern boundary.

⑰ The **Pool of Siloam** (cf. John 9:7), a focal point of Jerusalem, adjoined a large dam and reservoir, and received water from the Gihon Spring.

⑱ The **Hinnom Valley** was to the south of the hill that was the original city of David.

⑲ The **Upper City** housed luxurious villas of wealthy residents in the Herodian period.

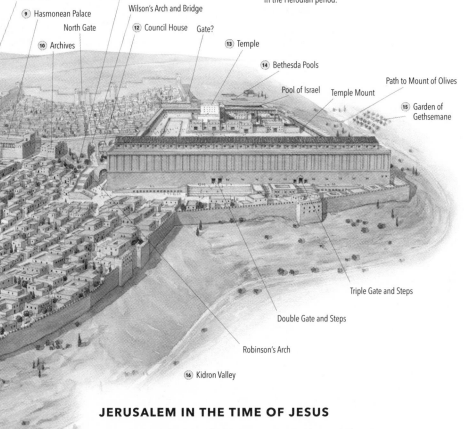

Second Wall

⑪ Xystus

Wilson's Arch and Bridge

⑨ Hasmonean Palace

North Gate

⑫ Council House

Gate?

⑩ Archives

⑬ Temple

⑭ Bethesda Pools

Pool of Israel

Temple Mount

Path to Mount of Olives

⑮ Garden of Gethsemane

Triple Gate and Steps

Double Gate and Steps

Robinson's Arch

⑯ Kidron Valley

JERUSALEM IN THE TIME OF JESUS

The heavily fortified city of Jerusalem lay atop adjacent hills in the mountainous region of Judea. It therefore proved difficult even for the Romans to recapture during the Jewish revolt, although they eventually did so in AD 70 after a bitter siege. The oldest portion of Jerusalem, called "the city of David" and "Mount Zion," lay to the south of the temple, but the city walls in the first century also encompassed the newer Upper City to the west of the temple. To the east, across the Kidron Valley (John 18:1), stood the Mount of Olives (Mark 13:3). To the south of Zion lay the Hinnom Valley. The reconstruction above depicts Jerusalem around AD 30, and the general direction of the drawing is looking north.

THE TEMPLE MOUNT IN THE TIME OF JESUS

Herod's Temple Mount was the focal point of Jerusalem during the time of Jesus. Sitting atop Jerusalem's northeastern ridge, it occupied one-sixth of the city's area. Under Herod the Great, the Temple Mount's foundation was expanded to encompass approximately 1.5 million square feet (140,000 square meters). Its foundational walls were constructed using gigantic stones, the largest found being 45 feet long, 11.5 feet high, and 12 feet thick (13.7 m by 3.5 m by 3.7 m).

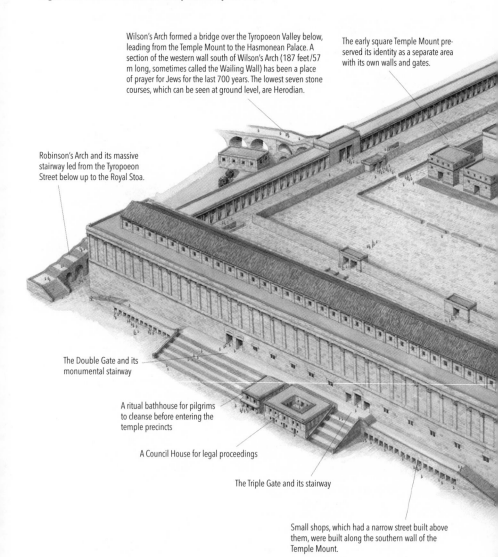

Wilson's Arch formed a bridge over the Tyropoeon Valley below, leading from the Temple Mount to the Hasmonean Palace. A section of the western wall south of Wilson's Arch (187 feet/57 m long, sometimes called the Wailing Wall) has been a place of prayer for Jews for the last 700 years. The lowest seven stone courses, which can be seen at ground level, are Herodian.

The early square Temple Mount preserved its identity as a separate area with its own walls and gates.

Robinson's Arch and its massive stairway led from the Tyropoeon Street below up to the Royal Stoa.

The Double Gate and its monumental stairway

A ritual bathhouse for pilgrims to cleanse before entering the temple precincts

A Council House for legal proceedings

The Triple Gate and its stairway

Small shops, which had a narrow street built above them, were built along the southern wall of the Temple Mount.

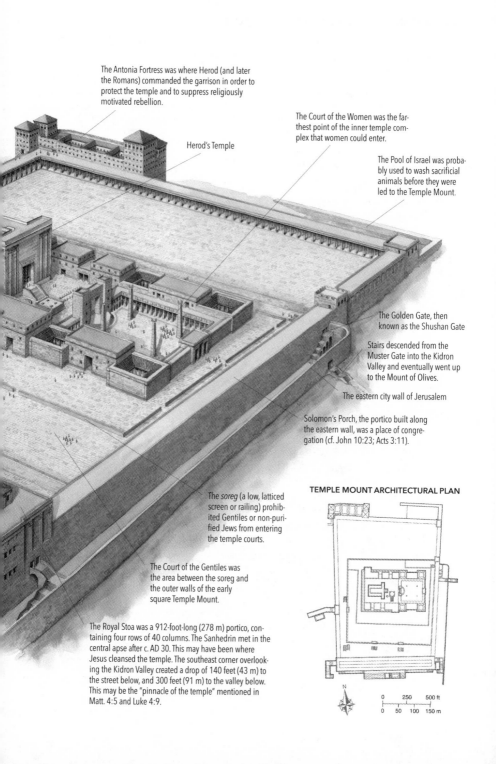

The Antonia Fortress was where Herod (and later the Romans) commanded the garrison in order to protect the temple and to suppress religiously motivated rebellion.

Herod's Temple

The Court of the Women was the farthest point of the inner temple complex that women could enter.

The Pool of Israel was probably used to wash sacrificial animals before they were led to the Temple Mount.

The Golden Gate, then known as the Shushan Gate

Stairs descended from the Muster Gate into the Kidron Valley and eventually went up to the Mount of Olives.

The eastern city wall of Jerusalem

Solomon's Porch, the portico built along the eastern wall, was a place of congregation (cf. John 10:23; Acts 3:11).

The *soreg* (a low, latticed screen or railing) prohibited Gentiles or non-purified Jews from entering the temple courts.

The Court of the Gentiles was the area between the soreg and the outer walls of the early square Temple Mount.

The Royal Stoa was a 912-foot-long (278 m) portico, containing four rows of 40 columns. The Sanhedrin met in the central apse after c. AD 30. This may have been where Jesus cleansed the temple. The southeast corner overlooking the Kidron Valley created a drop of 140 feet (43 m) to the street below, and 300 feet (91 m) to the valley below. This may be the "pinnacle of the temple" mentioned in Matt. 4:5 and Luke 4:9.

TEMPLE MOUNT ARCHITECTURAL PLAN

N

0	250	500 ft
0	50 100 150 m	

GOLGOTHA AND THE TEMPLE MOUNT

For many centuries, Christians have worshiped at the Church of the Holy Sepulchre in the belief that this was the place where Jesus was crucified, buried, and rose from the dead. This view was challenged in 1883 by General Charles Gordon, who argued that the Garden Tomb, a site just north of the Old City of Jerusalem, was the true site of Calvary.

According to the biblical writers, the requirements of the site were that it was outside the walls of Jerusalem at the time (Heb. 13:12), in a garden (John 19:41), near the city (John 19:20), and called Golgotha, meaning "Place of a Skull" (Matt. 27:33).

In the 1960s, excavations were carried out below the Church of the Holy Sepulchre, showing that it was built on an isolated mass of rock in the middle of an extensive quarry (which was in use from the eighth until the first century BC). This spur of rock was left unquarried in ancient times, because of the poor quality of the limestone. In the sides of the quarry and of

this rock, a series of rock-cut tombs of the style of the first century AD were found.

This would indicate that the area was not then included within the city walls, as the dead were always buried outside the city. In support of the second and third points, some fortified remains found in the northern part of the nearby Jewish Quarter excavations have been identified as the Gennath (Garden) Gate mentioned by Josephus in his description of the Second Wall (*Jewish War* 5.146). It is assumed that this gate derived its name from a garden which lay just to the north outside the gate. Indeed, a layer of arable soil was found above the quarry fill.

The claim that the site could have been known as "the place of a skull" is said to be based on an ancient Jewish tradition reported by early Christian writers, such as Origen and Epiphanius, that the skull of Adam is preserved in this hill.

General Gordon's identification of the Garden Tomb with that of Christ was based on his dis-

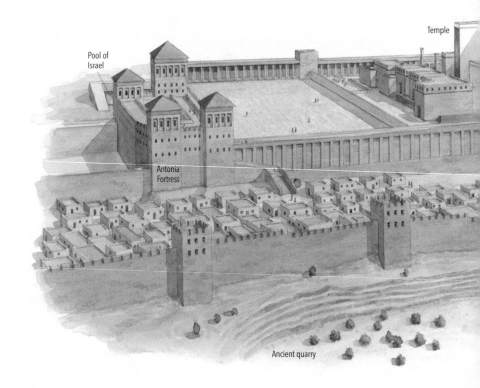

Temple

Pool of Israel

Antonia Fortress

Ancient quarry

cernment of the shape of a skull in the contours of the hill on the western escarpment of which the Garden Tomb is located. It has since been proven that this tomb was, in fact, a typical tomb of the First Temple period and could never have been called a "new tomb" in the time of Christ. Because of its tranquility, however, and its contrast to the bustle of the Holy Sepulchre, the site is today still regarded by many as the tomb of Christ.

The reconstruction drawing shows the traditional site of the crucifixion (i.e., the Holy Sepulchre). Three crosses are shown on the Hill of Golgotha. The Second Wall of Jerusalem was built above the quarry face. The Temple Mount forms the backdrop to this view, with the Antonia Fortress on the left, the temple in the center, and the Royal Stoa on the far right.

ARCHITECTURAL PLAN OF THE TEMPLE MOUNT

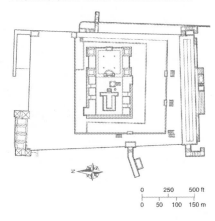

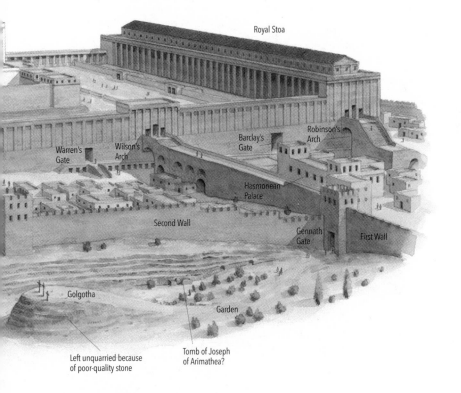

The Tomb of Jesus

The Gospel writers tell us that after his death, Jesus's body was taken to a garden and laid in a newly hewn tomb (Matt. 27:60; Luke 23:53; John 19:41). This is important archaeological information. Tombs from this period usually consisted of several burial chambers, which had *loculi* (burial niches) cut in the side walls in which to place the body of the deceased, and also *arcosolia* (arched niches) where ossuaries (chests for bones) were placed.

The fact that some women saw where the body of Jesus was laid (Mark 15:47) and that also, after the resurrection of Jesus, the disciple John could see the grave clothes lying and the face cloth folded (John 20:5–6), indicates that the body of Jesus was laid on a bench opposite the tomb opening.

The truth of this information can be confirmed by archaeology, in particular by tomb architecture. Newly hewn tombs usually consisted of a simple chamber which had three benches around an excavated pit. This pit allowed the workmen to stand upright while working.

Additional chambers with *loculi* and *arcosolia* were added later after the initial benches were removed. A newly hewn tomb could be used for the "primary burial," which is the first part of the ritual of ossilegium. (This simply means that the body of the deceased, after having been wrapped in linen grave clothes, was placed on a shelf, a bench, or in a niche. About a year later, after the soft tissues had decomposed, the bones were placed in an ossuary. This is called the "secondary burial.") It would appear, therefore, that the body of Jesus was indeed laid in a tomb that was newly hewn out of the rock.

The entrance to the tomb would have been low, causing the disciples to stoop down in order to look inside and enter it (cf. Luke 24:12; John 20:5). Only very few of the almost 1,000 excavated tombs of this period in and around Jerusalem had rolling stones to close off the entrance to the tomb. This luxury was restricted to the wealthy. Usually, tomb entrances had square or rectangular closing stones. These stones fit like a cork in a bottle in the tomb opening. The narrow part fit exactly in the inner opening, while the wider part closed off the outer opening.

However, the biblical record does say that the stone was rolled away (Matt. 27:60; Mark 15:46; Luke 24:2), and therefore a massive rolling stone (4.5 feet/1.4 m in diameter) is shown in this reconstruction drawing. The rare rolling stone entrance would be consistent with the idea that Joseph of Arimathea was "a rich man" (cf. Matt. 27:57).

his sacrifice. He knew beforehand that he must die in order to fulfill his mission. Jesus could endure the pain, but the terrifying weight of utter separation from God and God-forsakenness are something he has never experienced before and which, in the actual moment of suffering, seem unbearable.

Since the Aramaic word for God (*'Eli*) sounds similar to the Hebrew name Elijah (*'Eliyahu*), some of the bystanders interpret Jesus's cry as a request for help from Elijah and express curiosity: will Elijah actually come and save Jesus before he dies?[106] Jesus knows that the end is near and in order to fulfill Scripture says, "I thirst." This was likely to fulfill Psalm 69:21, which states, "And for my thirst they gave me sour wine to drink," although Psalm 22:15 also speaks of the sufferer's thirst. In response to Jesus's statement, an individual rushes to bring Jesus a drink in the form of a sponge filled with sour wine, a common and cheap drink.[107] Jesus may have been requesting a drink in order to triumphantly utter his final words.

Despite the onlookers' speculation that Elijah might come to rescue Jesus, this is not to be the case, and after crying out with a loud voice, Jesus dies.[108] Luke and John both provide statements that may have been the content of the final loud voice recorded in Matthew and Mark. Luke notes that Jesus prays, "Father, into your hands I commit my spirit!"[109] Jesus's faith in God remains strong even in the midst of death.[110] John records that before dying Jesus utters the phrase, "It is finished," indicating that the work for which he had come to earth has finally been fully accomplished— there is no longer any penalty left to be paid for sins.[111] Matthew and John describe Jesus as giving up his spirit, a description indicating that, even in his death, Jesus retains control.[112]

---

[106] Matthew 27:49; Mark 15:36.
[107] Matthew 27:47–48; Mark 15:35–36; John 19:29.
[108] Matthew 27:50; Mark 15:37; Luke 23:46.
[109] Luke 23:46.
[110] This observation is all the more poignant coming so closely on the heels of the cry of dereliction. Jesus prays the bedtime prayer of a young Jewish child to the very God whose absence he has just powerfully and abruptly felt.
[111] John 19:30.
[112] Matthew 27:50; John 19:30.

The Gospels mention several of Jesus's followers who apparently observed the crucifixion. Apart from Mary, Jesus's mother (whom, as mentioned, Jesus entrusted to the beloved disciple), these included Mary Magdalene, Mary the mother of James and Joses, Mary the wife of Clopas, and Salome the mother of the sons of Zebedee (i.e., James and John).[113] These were devoted women who had followed Jesus from Galilee and had financially supported him and his disciples.[114]

Supernatural Phenomena

Several supernatural phenomena accompany Jesus's death. First, the curtain of the temple tears in two from top to bottom.[115] This curtain separating the Holy Place from the Most Holy Place was 60 feet high and 30 feet wide and was only passed once a year by the high priest on the Day of Atonement. The supernatural tearing of this massive curtain indicates that God's people will now have direct access to his presence through Jesus, and Jesus's once-for-all sacrificial death has made animal sacrifices in the temple obsolete.[116]

Second, an earthquake shakes the area with enough force to split rocks.[117] Earthquakes were not uncommon in Palestine, but the particular timing of this earthquake would have seemed quite uncanny and unnerving to unbelieving observers, while believers would have interpreted the earthquake as a divine sign of God's judgment.

Third, Matthew alone records that many deceased saints rise from the dead and appear to many in Jerusalem after Jesus's resurrection.[118] Matthew is tantalizingly brief concerning the explicit details surrounding this event, and we are left with many unanswered questions. These Old Testament or intertestamental

---

[113] Matthew 27:56; Mark 15:40–41; Luke 23:49; John 20:1–18 (see also Luke 8:2–3). See the glossary for descriptions of each of these women.
[114] See Luke 8:1–3.
[115] Matthew 27:51; Mark 15:38; Luke 23:45.
[116] See Hebrews 9:11–10:22.
[117] Matthew 27:51.
[118] Matthew 27:52–53.

believers apparently receive resurrection bodies (unlike Lazarus who came back to life only to die again), bear witness to Christ's resurrection, and ascend to heaven sometime leading up to Jesus's ascension.

When the centurion and those keeping watch over Jesus see the earthquake and accompanying supernatural phenomena, Jesus's love for his tormentors, and the way Jesus died with a loud cry of prayer to God, they are filled with amazement and exclaim, "Truly this was the Son of God!"[119] A Roman centurion, of all people, uttering this confession proves particularly poignant as the climax of Mark's Gospel, which likely was written to the church in Rome. Luke notes that the centurion also says, "Certainly this man was innocent!"[120] Luke also provides the additional detail that after Jesus's death many of the spectators leave, beating their breasts—a symbolic action indicating grief and repentance.[121]

Soldiers Pierce Jesus's Side

John alone records two final details of Jesus's death that fulfilled Scripture.[122] Because the crucifixion occurred on the day of Preparation for the Sabbath of Passover week ("a high day"), the Jewish leaders ask Pilate to break the legs of the criminals so that their bodies can be taken down before the Sabbath (which began at nightfall on Friday night, perhaps around 7:00 p.m.). According to Deuteronomy 21:22–23, the bodies of hanged criminals defiled the land by remaining on a tree overnight, and the Jewish leaders do not want any such defilement to hang over Jerusalem during Passover week. Pilate complies with their request, and the soldiers proceed to break the legs of the two robbers who have been crucified with Jesus. This ensures rapid death from asphyxiation because the crucified ones are no longer able to push themselves up to breathe.

When the soldiers approach Jesus, they realize that he has

---

[119] Matthew 27:54; Mark 15:39.
[120] Luke 23:47.
[121] Luke 23:48.
[122] John 19:31–37.

already died and therefore do not bother breaking his legs. John does not indicate the motive, but he notes that one soldier instead takes a spear and pierces Jesus's side with it, releasing a flow of blood and water. After affirming the truthfulness of his account, John proceeds to note the two scriptural prophecies fulfilled by these final actions. First, the fact that the soldiers did not break Jesus's legs fulfilled Psalm 34:20, which claims, "He keeps all his bones; not one of them is broken." Second, the fact that a Roman soldier pierced Jesus's side with a spear fulfilled Zechariah 12:10, where the prophet writes, speaking of a divine suffering figure, "When they look on me, on him whom they have pierced, they shall mourn for him."

THE BURIAL OF JESUS

Joseph of Arimathea buries Jesus in a new tomb.

MATTHEW 27:57-61

When it was evening, there came a rich man from Arimathea, named Joseph, who also was a disciple of Jesus. He went to Pilate and asked for the body of Jesus. Then Pilate ordered it to be given to him. And Joseph took the body and wrapped it in a clean linen shroud and laid it in his own new tomb, which he had cut in the rock. And he rolled a great stone to the entrance of the tomb and went away. Mary Magdalene and the other Mary were there, sitting opposite the tomb.

MARK 15:42-47

And when evening had come, since it was the day of Preparation, that is, the day before the Sabbath, Joseph of Arimathea, a respected member of the council, who was also himself looking for the kingdom of God, took courage and went to Pilate and asked for the body of Jesus. Pilate was surprised to hear that he should have already died. And summoning the centurion, he asked him whether he was already dead. And when he learned from the centurion that he was dead, he granted the corpse to Joseph. And Joseph bought a linen shroud, and taking him down, wrapped him in the linen shroud and laid him in a tomb that had been cut out of the rock. And he rolled a stone against the entrance of the tomb. Mary Magdalene and Mary the mother of Joses saw where he was laid.

LUKE 23:50-56

Now there was a man named Joseph, from the Jewish town of Arimathea. He was a member of the council, a good and righteous man, who had not consented to their decision and action; and he was looking for the kingdom of God. This man went to Pilate and asked for the body of Jesus. Then he took it down and wrapped it in a linen shroud and laid him in a tomb cut in stone, where no one had ever yet been laid. It was the day of Preparation, and the Sabbath was beginning. The women who had come with him from Galilee followed and saw the tomb and how his body was laid. Then they returned and prepared spices and ointments.

On the Sabbath they rested according to the commandment.

JOHN 19:38-42

After these things Joseph of Arimathea, who was a disciple of Jesus, but secretly for fear of the Jews, asked Pilate that he might take away the body of Jesus, and Pilate gave him permission. So he came and took away his body. Nicodemus also, who earlier had come to Jesus by night, came bringing a mixture of myrrh and aloes, about seventy-five pounds in weight. So they took the body of Jesus and bound it in linen cloths with the spices, as is the burial custom of the Jews. Now in the place where he was crucified there was a garden, and in the garden a new tomb in which no one had yet been laid. So because of the Jewish day of Preparation, since the tomb was close at hand, they laid Jesus there.

COMMENTARY

When evening approaches, Joseph of Arimathea asks Pilate for permission to bury the body of Jesus. No mention is made of Joseph prior to this point in the narrative, but the four Gospels paint a brief yet vivid portrait.[123] Joseph was a rich man who was a member of the Sanhedrin and a secret disciple of Jesus. While being a high-standing member of the Jewish community, he had not consented to the ruling Council's decision. Joseph was a good and righteous man who was actively looking for the kingdom of God. His request to bury Jesus required a good deal of courage, since it makes his sympathy for Jesus public at a time when such sympathy could be dangerous.[124]

Mark notes that Pilate is quite surprised that Jesus is already dead. It normally took much longer to die on a cross, but after confirming Jesus's death with the centurion, Pilate grants Joseph's request to bury the body.[125] It is important for Joseph to bury Jesus's body quickly, because Deuteronomy 21:23 commands that a corpse be buried on the day of death. The time constraints are intensified because Sabbath started at sundown of Friday evening.

Joseph purchases a linen shroud, wraps Jesus's body in it, and lays the body in his own newly cut tomb nearby.[126] Rock-cut tombs were very expensive and labor intensive and generally belonged to wealthy families; the tomb was likely Joseph's family tomb. He finishes the hasty burial by rolling a stone against the entrance. Archaeological evidence confirms that circular stones were occasionally used to seal tombs during this time period, although square or rectangular stones were much more common. The main purpose of the stone was to keep wild animals from devouring the body. John notes that Nicodemus assists Joseph in the burial by providing approximately 75 pounds of myrrh and aloes to wrap the body in the linen, an extravagant gesture indicating the high esteem in

---

[123] Matthew 27:57; Mark 15:43; Luke 23:50–51; John 19:38.
[124] Compare the reaction of the disciples who met behind locked doors out of fear of the Jewish authorities (John 21:19, 26).
[125] Mark 15:44–45.
[126] Matthew 27:59–60; Mark 15:46; Luke 23:53; John 19:40–41.

which Nicodemus held Jesus.[127] The burial of Jesus in the tomb of a rich man confirms Isaiah's prophecy, "And they made his grave with the wicked and with a rich man in his death" (Isa. 53:9a).

Matthew, Mark, and Luke conclude their accounts of Jesus's burial by noting that Mary Magdalene and Mary the mother of Joses observe Jesus's burial and know the tomb in which he is laid.[128] Believing that the body has been insufficiently prepared because of the hasty burial, these women pay careful attention to the location, intending to return after the Sabbath with additional spices and ointments.[129]

---

[127] John 19:39–40. Ordinary people were normally buried in the ground, not in a tomb. The bodies were wrapped in linen shrouds with the preservatives, and when the body had decayed, the bones would be placed in an ossuary.
[128] Matthew 27:61; Mark 15:47; Luke 23:55.
[129] Luke 23:55–56.

SATURDAY

APRIL 4, AD 33

THE JEWISH LEADERS POST GUARDS

The chief priests and Pharisees place guards at the tomb with Pilate's permission.

MATTHEW 27:62-66

The next day, that is, after the day of Preparation, the chief priests and the Pharisees gathered before Pilate and said,

> "Sir, we remember how that impostor said, while he was still alive,
>
>> 'After three days I will rise.'
>
> Therefore order the tomb to be made secure until the third day, lest his disciples go and steal him away and tell the people,
>
>> 'He has risen from the dead,'
>
> and the last fraud will be worse than the first."

Pilate said to them,

> "You have a guard of soldiers. Go, make it as secure as you can."

So they went and made the tomb secure by sealing the stone and setting a guard.

COMMENTARY

The Gospels do not provide any information concerning the activity of the disciples on the Sabbath (Friday sundown to Saturday sundown). We can presume, however, based upon their actions Sunday evening—fearfully hiding together behind locked doors— that Saturday was spent in secretive fear and dread. The disciples are reeling from the shock of the previous day's rapid events. They had devoted their lives to following a person who had been brutally and shamefully executed as a criminal. Their hopes for the establishment of God's messianic kingdom lie shattered like so many pieces of broken pottery. They are likely sleep-deprived and terrified of pursuit and prosecution by the Jewish leaders. With their leader executed for fomenting political sedition, they have good reason to be afraid. With Jerusalem still overrun with thousands of Passover pilgrims, it would have been relatively easy to blend in and disappear; some may have fled to Bethany or elsewhere before sundown Friday. Luke's statement, "On the Sabbath they rested according to the commandment" (Luke 23:56), may veil the emotional and physical turmoil of Jesus's followers on the day following the crucifixion.

Matthew alone records activity on Saturday. The chief priests and Pharisees approach Pilate and ask him to secure the tomb until the third day (i.e., Sunday).[1] They explain to Pilate that the "impostor" had said, "After three days I will rise," and they express concern that if the disciples stole the body and proclaim a resurrection, "the last fraud will be worse than the first."[2] The fact that the Jewish leaders send this delegation to Pilate on the Sabbath reveals their perception of the situation—they are afraid as well. Their fear may have been exacerbated by the unusual circumstances surrounding Jesus's death: the darkness, the tearing of the temple curtain, and the earthquake. Would Jesus's death take care of the problem or make things worse? Jesus had made several predictions of his resurrection, which his disciples either failed to

---

[1] The reckoning of days was not necessarily in twenty-four-hour blocks but included parts of days.
[2] Matthew 27:63–64.

understand or had difficulty believing.[3] The Jewish leaders have heard rumors of these predictions (or may even have heard them from Jesus himself) and want to ensure that Jesus's disciples do not perpetrate a hoax by making it appear that the predictions have come true. They, along with the disciples themselves, apparently had no expectation of a genuine supernatural resurrection.

Pilate's response is hard to interpret. He could be granting the Jewish authorities permission and providing them with a guard of Roman soldiers from the Roman military guard assigned to temple security, or he could be denying their request and telling them to guard the tomb with their own Jewish temple police.[4] Either way, he acquiesces to their desire to secure the tomb, and they respond by sealing the stone and setting a guard, perhaps made up of both Roman and Jewish security forces.

---

[3] Mark 8:31; 9:31; 10:34.
[4] The Greek in Matthew 27:65 could be translated as either "you have a guard" or "have a guard."

SUNDAY

WOMEN DISCOVER THE EMPTY TOMB

Some women discover the empty tomb and are instructed by angels.

MATTHEW 28:1-7

Now after the Sabbath, toward the dawn of the first day of the week, Mary Magdalene and the other Mary went to see the tomb.

And behold, there was a great earthquake, for an angel of the Lord descended from heaven and came and rolled back the stone and sat on it.

His appearance was like lightning, and his clothing white as snow.

And for fear of him the guards trembled and became like dead men.

But the angel said to the women,

> "Do not be afraid, for I know that you seek Jesus who was crucified.
>
> He is not here, for he has risen, as he said.
>
> Come, see the place where he lay.
>
> Then go quickly and tell his disciples that he has risen from the dead, and behold, he is going before you to Galilee; there you will see him.
>
> See, I have told you."

MARK 16:1-7

When the Sabbath was past, Mary Magdalene, Mary the mother of James, and Salome bought spices, so that they might go and anoint him.

And very early on the first day of the week, when the sun had risen, they went to the tomb. And they were saying to one another,

> "Who will roll away the stone for us from the entrance of the tomb?"

And looking up, they saw that the stone had been rolled back—it was very large.

And entering the tomb, they saw a young man sitting on the right side, dressed in a white robe, and they were alarmed.

And he said to them,

> "Do not be alarmed.
>
> You seek Jesus of Nazareth, who was crucified.
>
> He has risen; he is not here.
>
> See the place where they laid him.
>
> But go, tell his disciples and Peter that he is going before you to Galilee.
>
> There you will see him, just as he told you."

LUKE 24:1-7

But on the first day of the week, at early dawn, they [i.e., the women of Luke 23:55] went to the tomb, taking the spices they had prepared.

And they found the stone rolled away from the tomb, but when they went in they did not find the body of the Lord Jesus.

While they were perplexed about this, behold, two men stood by them in dazzling apparel.

And as they were frightened and bowed their faces to the ground, the men said to them,

> "Why do you seek the living among the dead?
>
> He is not here, but has risen.
>
> Remember how he told you, while he was still in Galilee, that the Son of Man must be delivered into the hands of sinful men and be crucified and on the third day rise."

JOHN 20:1

Now on the first day of the week Mary Magdalene came to the tomb early, while it was still dark, and saw that the stone had been taken away from the tomb.

COMMENTARY

Human experience consistently confirms the fact that death is final and irreversible. Nothing changes this—nothing natural, that is. But what of the supernatural? Could God raise his Messiah from the dead? Despite Jesus's predictions, his own disciples do not seem to expect that God will do so. Death by crucifixion is too great an obstacle—it has completely overturned all of their preconceived messianic expectations. There is no way God's true Messiah could die like that. After all, hadn't Yahweh revealed in his authoritative law that those who died on a tree like this are either blasphemers or traitors (Deut. 21:22–23)? If Matthew had ended at chapter 27, Mark at chapter 15, Luke at chapter 23, and John at chapter 19, this would indeed be the end of the story. Jesus would have been just another failed messianic pretender who clashed with the Roman Empire and paid the ultimate price for his folly. Each Gospel, however, adds an additional chapter (or, in the case of John, two) that changes everything. The story is not yet over, and the world is about to be turned upside down. New creation is about to break into the midst of this old creation, and nothing will ever be the same.

The resurrection accounts have often been excoriated by crit-ics of Christianity as being contradictory. How many women went to the tomb? How many angels were there? To whom did Jesus appear, and when? However, while the Gospel narratives are dif-ferent, they are not contradictory. They reflect exactly what we would expect from eyewitness accounts of such an unexpected and supernatural event. Their very differences confirm the truthful-ness of the resurrection. If the disciples had stolen the body and created a conspiracy to deceive the masses, they surely would have created more uniform accounts, and they most certainly would not have posited women as the first eyewitnesses. In first-century Palestine, the testimony of women was easily dismissed and car-ried little weight.[1]

The differences between the Gospel accounts attest to multiple independent eyewitnesses, each of whom communicated particu-lar details from their individual perspectives. The differences will be discussed below, but it is important to stress at the outset that none of the differences represents an irreconcilable contradiction.

The Resurrection

Matthew alone seems to record the events associated with the actual resurrection.[2] An angel of the Lord, accompanied by a great earthquake, descends like lightning, rolls the stone back, and sits on it. The soldiers who have been guarding the tomb are terrified and become "like dead men."[3] Matthew does not explicitly state that Jesus arose from the dead at this time, but he had at least been raised by now.

Matthew also does not indicate any break in time between verses 4 and 5, but upon the basis of the other Gospels it is safe to infer that several things take place between the appearance of the angel to the guards and the arrival of the women. The guards ap-parently come to their senses enough to flee, and the angel moves

---

[1] Some claim there is little evidence for this claim, but it is supported by Jewish texts such as Pseudo-Philo, *Liber Antiquitatum Biblicarum* 9:10; 42:1–5; *Leviticus Rabbah* 10:5.
[2] Matthew 28:2–4.
[3] Matthew 28:4.

from the stone to inside the tomb, since the other Gospels do not describe the women meeting the guards or seeing an angel outside the tomb. The fact that Matthew does not record a break in time between verses 4 and 5 fits the style of his account of the resurrection, which is quite abbreviated in comparison to Luke and John.

Matthew may have drawn his account of the descent of the angel and the rolling away of the stone from the eyewitness report of one of the Roman or Jewish temple guards who were present at the event or from one of the believing members of the Sanhedrin. This would explain his particular knowledge (contained in 28:11–15) of the activity of these guards after they fled the tomb. The guards go first to the chief priests who proceed to bribe the soldiers with money and promise to shield them from Pilate's wrath—a promise that would have been quite persuasive to the guards since dereliction of duty could have been punished by execution—if they agree to spread the lie that the disciples stole the body during the night while they were sleeping. The guards readily agree, and their account of the events "has been spread among the Jews to this day" (i.e., the late AD 50s or early 60s when Matthew likely wrote his Gospel).[4] The cover-up successfully deceived some despite the inherent improbabilities. Would all the guards really have fallen asleep? How would they have known it was the disciples if they were sleeping? Would the sound of the stone being rolled away not have woken them up?

The Empty Tomb

Matthew records that Mary Magdalene and the other Mary go to the tomb near dawn on Sunday (perhaps between 6:00 and 6:15 a.m.).[5] They encounter an angel who commands them not to fear, informs them Jesus is not in the tomb, invites them to look around the tomb for his body, and commands them to go tell his disciples that Jesus has risen from the dead and will meet them in Galilee.[6]

---

[4] Matthew 28:15.
[5] Matthew 28:1.
[6] Matthew 28:5–7.

Mark records that Mary Magdalene, Mary the mother of James, and Salome buy spices after the Sabbath (Saturday night) and go early on Sunday morning to the tomb to anoint Jesus's body in keeping with Jewish burial customs, which had not been properly carried out due to the haste of the burial on Friday afternoon.[7] On the way, they discuss how they will get past the large stone, but upon arriving at the tomb they find the stone rolled away. When they enter the tomb, they see a young man sitting on the right side and are alarmed, but the man instructs them not to be concerned; Jesus has risen and is not there, and they are to go tell his disciples, and Peter in particular, that he will meet them in Galilee.[8]

Luke records that Mary Magdalene, Joanna, Mary the mother of James, and at least two other unnamed women go to the tomb at early dawn on Sunday with the spices they had prepared.[9] When they arrive, they discover that the stone has been rolled away and that Jesus's body is missing. Two men in dazzling apparel appear and speak to the frightened women. They ask the women why they are looking for the living among the dead, inform them that Jesus has risen, and remind them of Jesus's prior prediction of his crucifixion and resurrection.[10] The angel's announcement jogs the women's memories, and they remember Jesus's words.

John records that Mary Magdalene goes to the tomb while it is still dark Sunday morning, sees the stone rolled away, and flees the scene to report what she has seen to the disciples.[11] She later returns to the tomb following Peter and John and encounters Jesus (John 20:11–18). In her report to the disciples in John 20:2, she says, "We [plural] do not know where they have laid him," implying the presence of other women. Authors commonly refer only to

---

[7] Mark 16:1. Luke 23:55 records that at least some of the women prepared some of the spices and ointments from their personal supply late Friday afternoon before the Sabbath.
[8] Mark 16:5–7. Mark's particular reference to Peter likely results from Peter's personal remembrance, since according to the early church fathers the Gospel of Mark was based upon Peter's teaching and preaching.
[9] Luke 24:1, 10.
[10] Luke 24:4–8.
[11] John 20:1–2. The description of Mary Magdalene going while it was still dark fits with the other Gospels' presentation of early morning. It is possible that the women began their journey while it was still dark and arrived just as the sun was coming up as described in Mark 16:2 or that Mary went to the tomb alone while it was still dark before the other women arrived.

the most prominent member of a group (Mary Magdalene in this case) and do not note the presence of other minor characters. Mary Magdalene, being mentioned first in the other Gospel accounts, was the best known of the early female witnesses; perhaps she was still alive and active in some part of the early church when the Gospels first began to circulate.

There is not enough information to decide precisely how John's account fits with those in the other Gospels. Several scenarios are possible. Most probably, the women all went together, and upon seeing the stone rolled away, Mary Magdalene immediately fled to tell the disciples while the other women went into the tomb and were greeted by the angels. The ignorance of Mary's report that Jesus's body had been moved (John 20:2) and her grief and tears upon returning to the tomb (John 20:11) indicate that she had not heard the angels' reassuring report that Jesus had risen. Alternatively, Mary Magdalene may have initially gone to the garden by herself, found the tomb empty, and fled to tell the disciples, while the other women arrived shortly thereafter. In this case, the inclusion of Mary in the other Gospel accounts may be due to an abbreviated conflation of the trips of the various women to the tomb. Another possibility is that if Mary Magdalene initially went to the tomb alone, her second trip to the tomb recorded in John could correspond to the visit of the women to the tomb recorded in the other three Gospels.[12]

The slight differences between the words of the angel at the tomb reflect the selectivity of each individual Gospel author. None of the authors claims to record every word that was spoken, and the words are complementary, not contradictory. Only a hardened skeptic would insist that the angel could not have said everything recorded in Matthew, Mark, and Luke. The difference in the number of angels (one or two) inside the tomb is easily explained by the fact that one angel was more prominent and did all the talk-

---

[12]Other hypothetical reconstructions are possible based upon the reports contained in the four Gospels, but there is no need to spend more time on the possibilities because the main point is that there are no irreconcilable contradictions. The four Gospel authors are selectively relating the main facts, condensing some of the material, and possibly topically arranging other material in full compliance with acceptable standards of ancient historiography.

ing while the other angel remained silent. Matthew and Mark do not say only one angel was present, and there was no need to be more specific, because the focus of the narrative is on what the angel had to say and not how many were there. No author claims to communicate every possible detail.

———•◦•———

THE WOMEN TELL THE DISCIPLES

The women, fearful and joyful, leave the garden and tell the disciples.

MATTHEW 28:8-10

So they departed quickly from the tomb with fear and great joy, and ran to tell his disciples.

And behold, Jesus met them and said,

"Greetings!"

And they came up and took hold of his feet and worshiped him.

Then Jesus said to them,

"Do not be afraid; go and tell my brothers to go to Galilee, and there they will see me."

MARK 16:8

And they went out and fled from the tomb, for trembling and astonishment had seized them, and they said nothing to anyone, for they were afraid.

LUKE 24:8-11

And they remembered his words, and returning from the tomb they told all these things to the eleven and to all the rest.

Now it was Mary Magdalene and Joanna and Mary the mother of James and the other women with them who told these things to the apostles, but these words seemed to them an idle tale, and they did not believe them.

JOHN 20:2

So she ran and went to Simon Peter and the other disciple, the one whom Jesus loved, and said to them,

> "They have taken the Lord out of the tomb, and we do not know where they have laid him."

COMMENTARY

It is likely that Mary Magdalene either goes to the tomb alone before the others, sees the stone rolled away, assumes the body had been stolen, and rushes to tell Peter and John. Alternatively, she initially goes along with the other women, dashes off to tell Peter and John while the other women remain and encounter the angels in the tomb. Either way, the first report to some of the disciples on Sunday morning comes from a scared and sorrowful Mary Magdalene, who assumes the body has been moved (John 20:2).

Mark records the initial response of the other women to the angel's announcement and instructions: "And they went out and fled from the tomb, for trembling and astonishment had seized them, and they said nothing to anyone, for they were afraid."[13] Based upon the material in the other Gospels, it is evident that the women's silence does not last long. They are initially afraid and joyful (such a supernatural occurrence is surely capable of producing both emotions at once) but soon find their way back to the disciples to report what the angel had said.[14] Matthew records how Jesus appears to the women as they are traveling to tell the disciples; they worship him, and he instructs them not to be afraid but to tell the disciples to meet him in Galilee (120 miles or so to

---

[13] Mark 16:8. It is very likely that the original text of the Gospel of Mark ended at verse 8 or had an ending that was subsequently lost or destroyed. Mark 16:9–20 was in all probability not part of the original text.

[14] Matthew 28:8; Luke 24:9.

the north, avoiding a route through Samaria).[15] The fact that the women touched his feet indicates that he was not a mirage or hallucination but rather a physical body. What is more, Jesus does not refuse their worship—underscoring his divinity, since only God alone is worthy of worship—a truth for which many first-century Jews were willing to die.[16] Although Matthew does not provide the details, it is possible that this meeting took place after the women gave their report to Peter and John and as they were traveling to tell the disciples in Bethany, where many of them (minus Peter and John) had likely fled early Friday morning.

It is likely that Mary Magdalene gives her report and slowly begins making her way back to the tomb to mourn, as she is described as doing in John 20:11. Peter and John appear to delay their rush to the tomb and do not set out until they receive the further report from the women who had seen the angels (Luke 24:12).[17] The disciples do not believe the initial report from the women and view it as an "idle tale" (Luke 24:11), but Peter and John decide to investigate the matter further and run to the tomb, possibly passing Mary on the way.[18]

PETER AND JOHN RUSH TO THE TOMB

Peter and John rush to the tomb based upon Mary Magdalene's report and discover it empty.

LUKE 24:12

But Peter rose and ran to the tomb; stooping and looking in, he saw the linen cloths by themselves; and he went home marveling at what had happened.

---

[15] Matthew 28:9–10.
[16] See Revelation 19:10.
[17] John's report does not require that the men departed immediately (John 20:2–3).
[18] There also would have been many possible ways to travel from the house where they were gathered to the tomb in the maze-like Jerusalem streets, and they may have passed Mary by taking a different route.

JOHN 20:3-10

So Peter went out with the other disciple, and they were going toward the tomb.

Both of them were running together, but the other disciple outran Peter and reached the tomb first.

And stooping to look in, he saw the linen cloths lying there, but he did not go in.

Then Simon Peter came, following him, and went into the tomb.

He saw the linen cloths lying there, and the face cloth, which had been on Jesus' head, not lying with the linen cloths but folded up in a place by itself.

Then the other disciple, who had reached the tomb first, also went in, and he saw and believed; for as yet they did not understand the Scripture, that he must rise from the dead.

Then the disciples went back to their homes.

COMMENTARY

Having received the report from the women—both Mary's initial fearful report that the body had been moved and the further report from the other women who had encountered the angels—Peter and John rush to the tomb to investigate the matter for themselves. Luke mentions only Peter's visit to the tomb, but John includes his own eyewitness information (he accompanied Peter).[19] The presence of two male witnesses to the empty tomb would have carried a great deal more weight in the first century, yet the Gospel authors strikingly do not alter the accounts to have the men discover the tomb first, encounter the angels, or see Jesus. Women were the first eyewitnesses of all these things—no one in the ancient world would have posited such eyewitnesses if they had wanted their

---

[19] Luke 24:12; John 20:3. Luke later indicates that he knew that more men besides Peter had gone to the tomb, when he records the disciples on the Emmaus road as saying, "*Some* of those who were with us went to the tomb and found it just as the women had said, but him they did not see" (Luke 24:24).

account to be believed. This fact strongly reinforces the historicity of the events recorded in the Gospels.

Many of the details recorded by John carry little theological weight but rather reflect John's eyewitness recollections: he outruns Peter; pauses at the opening; stoops to peer in; and enters only after Peter has gone into the tomb first. Other details are much more significant. The presence of the linen cloths and the face cloth folded up strongly point toward the reality of a supernatural resurrection. If grave robbers, the disciples, or Jesus's enemies had stolen the body, they would not have gone through the time-consuming effort of carefully removing and folding the linen cloths and face cloth only to carry away a naked corpse. What is more, grave robbers would not have left the most valuable material, the cloths and spices. John recounts how the sight of the linen cloths and face cloth caused him to believe even though none of the disciples yet understood how the Old Testament Scriptures pointed forward to Jesus's resurrection.

MARY RETURNS TO THE TOMB AND ENCOUNTERS JESUS

JOHN 20:11-18

But Mary stood weeping outside the tomb, and as she wept she stooped to look into the tomb.

And she saw two angels in white, sitting where the body of Jesus had lain, one at the head and one at the feet.

They said to her,

> "Woman, why are you weeping?"

She said to them,

> "They have taken away my Lord, and I do not know where they have laid him."

Having said this, she turned around and saw Jesus standing, but she did not know that it was Jesus.

Jesus said to her,

> "Woman, why are you weeping? Whom are you seeking?"

Supposing him to be the gardener, she said to him,

> "Sir, if you have carried him away, tell me where you have laid him, and I will take him away."

Jesus said to her,

> "Mary."

She turned and said to him in Aramaic,

> "Rabboni!" (which means Teacher).

Jesus said to her,

> "Do not cling to me, for I have not yet ascended to the Father; but go to my brothers and say to them,
>
>> 'I am ascending to my Father and your Father, to my God and your God.'"

Mary Magdalene went and announced to the disciples,

> "I have seen the Lord"

—and that he had said these things to her.

COMMENTARY

John alone records Mary's return to the tomb in the wake of Peter and John's visit in order to weep and mourn for Jesus.[20] In the course of her weeping, she peers into the tomb and is startled to see two angels sitting where Jesus's body had been. The angels ask her why she is weeping, and her reply indicates that she has not

---

[20] It is possible that this visit corresponds to the visit of the women recorded in the other Gospels examined above despite the fact that John does not mention the presence of other women, but this does not seem to be the most likely historical reconstruction.

yet heard the report from the other women: "They have taken away my Lord, and I do not know where they have laid him."[21] She turns around, perhaps after hearing someone approaching, and sees Jesus but does not recognize Jesus, just as the disciples on the road to Emmaus fail to initially recognize him.[22]

Jesus asks her why she is weeping and whom she is looking for. She assumes he is the gardener responsible for supervising the tombs and, thinking that he may have removed the body, perhaps because Jesus had been buried in the tomb of a wealthy family, she asks him where the body has been taken. At this point Jesus utters Mary's name, at which she immediately recognizes him, perhaps by the tone of his voice. He instructs her not to cling to him but to go to his "brothers"—the disciples—and to inform them that he is about to ascend to his Father and their Father, to his God and their God.[23] Such a way of describing his relationship to his followers communicates a deep degree of familial intimacy. Mary obediently responds by going and informing the disciples that she has seen Jesus and recounting what Jesus has said to her. This second report strongly contrasts with her first report of despair earlier that morning.

———— •◦• ————

ENCOUNTER ON EMMAUS ROAD

Jesus appears to Cleopas and a friend on the road to Emmaus.

LUKE 24:13-35

That very day two of them were going to a village named Emmaus, about seven miles from Jerusalem, and they were talking with each other about all these things that had happened. While they were talking and discussing together, Jesus himself drew near and went

---

[21] John 20:13.
[22] This failure to initially recognize Jesus in his resurrected body likely resulted from supernatural activity—God kept them from recognizing Jesus until the time was right.
[23] John 20:17.

with them. But their eyes were kept from recognizing him. And he said to them,

> "What is this conversation that you are holding with each other as you walk?"

And they stood still, looking sad. Then one of them, named Cleopas, answered him,

> "Are you the only visitor to Jerusalem who does not know the things that have happened there in these days?"

And he said to them,

> "What things?"

And they said to him,

> "Concerning Jesus of Nazareth, a man who was a prophet mighty in deed and word before God and all the people, and how our chief priests and rulers delivered him up to be condemned to death, and crucified him.
>
> But we had hoped that he was the one to redeem Israel.
>
> Yes, and besides all this, it is now the third day since these things happened.
>
> Moreover, some women of our company amazed us.
>
> They were at the tomb early in the morning, and when they did not find his body, they came back saying that they had even seen a vision of angels, who said that he was alive.
>
> Some of those who were with us went to the tomb and found it just as the women had said, but him they did not see."

And he said to them,

> "O foolish ones, and slow of heart to believe all that the prophets have spoken!
>
> Was it not necessary that the Christ should suffer these things and enter into his glory?"

And beginning with Moses and all the Prophets, he interpreted to them in all the Scriptures the things concerning himself.

So they drew near to the village to which they were going. He acted as if he were going farther, but they urged him strongly, saying,

> "Stay with us, for it is toward evening and the day is now far spent."

So he went in to stay with them. When he was at table with them, he took the bread and blessed and broke it and gave it to them. And their eyes were opened, and they recognized him. And he vanished from their sight. They said to each other,

> "Did not our hearts burn within us while he talked to us on the road, while he opened to us the Scriptures?"

And they rose that same hour and returned to Jerusalem. And they found the eleven and those who were with them gathered together, saying,

> "The Lord has risen indeed, and has appeared to Simon!"

Then they told what had happened on the road, and how he was known to them in the breaking of the bread.

COMMENTARY

Luke's account of Jesus's appearance to two disciples on the road to Emmaus—a town about seven miles northwest of Jerusalem—on Sunday afternoon is filled with comical irony and many fascinating features.[24] As with Mary, the disciples do not initially recognize Jesus when he begins to walk alongside them and engages them in conversation. When Jesus inquires concerning their conversation, they literally stop in their tracks, and Cleopas says, "Are you the only visitor to Jerusalem who does not know the things that

---

[24] It is often assumed that both travelers were men, but the text is not explicit, and it may have been Cleopas and his wife. This appearance of Jesus is briefly mentioned in Mark 16:12.

have happened there in these days?"[25] Jesus wants to hear their perspective and asks, "What things?"[26]

They answer Jesus in two parts. First, they give a brief history of the whole situation as it would likely have been perceived by the average sympathetic Jewish follower: Jesus of Nazareth was a mighty prophet before God and the people and had been condemned to death and crucified by the Jewish leaders and rulers, "but we had hoped that he was the one to redeem Israel."[27] Jesus was a mighty prophet whom many had hoped would be God's Messiah but who had been crucified by the powers that be. Second, Cleopas and the other disciple recount the unusual events that had transpired that morning: some women had found the tomb empty and had reported an amazing story of angels proclaiming Jesus's resurrection, and some men had investigated and found the tomb empty but did not see Jesus.

At this point, Jesus rebukes the two disciples for their slowness to believe in light of the prophecies concerning the Messiah's suffering and glorification, and "beginning with Moses and all the Prophets, he interpreted to them in all the Scriptures the things concerning himself."[28] Jesus is here remedying the problem identified by John when he notes, "For as yet they did not understand the Scripture, that he must rise from the dead" (John 20:9). The disciples had not been expecting the events of Easter morning.[29]

As they approach the village, Jesus acts as if he is traveling farther, and the two disciples urge him to stay with them for the evening. Jesus complies and at supper takes the bread and blesses it. At this point (perhaps having witnessed Jesus praying and blessing the food before a meal at a previous occasion), the eyes of Cleopas and the other disciple are divinely opened, they recognize Jesus, and he vanishes from their sight.

---

[25] Luke 24:18.
[26] Luke 24:19.
[27] Luke 24:21.
[28] Luke 24:27.
[29] Again, this strongly suggests that the Gospel accounts of Jesus's resurrection are historically accurate.

They immediately return to Jerusalem and find the disciples in intense conversation—at some earlier point in the day Jesus had also appeared to Peter! (This appearance to Peter is not described in the Gospels but is mentioned by Paul in 1 Corinthians 15:5.) After hearing of Jesus's amazing appearance to Peter, the two disciples proceed to describe how Jesus had spoken to them on the road and how they had recognized him when he broke the bread.[30]

JESUS APPEARS TO THE TEN WITHOUT THOMAS

That evening Jesus appears to the ten (minus Thomas) in a house in Jerusalem.

LUKE 24:36-43

As they were talking about these things, Jesus himself stood among them, and said to them,

"Peace to you!"

But they were startled and frightened and thought they saw a spirit.

And he said to them,

"Why are you troubled, and why do doubts arise in your hearts?

See my hands and my feet, that it is I myself.

Touch me, and see.

For a spirit does not have flesh and bones as you see that I have."

And when he had said this, he showed them his hands and his feet.

And while they still disbelieved for joy and were marveling, he said to them,

"Have you anything here to eat?"

---

[30] According to Mark 16:13, the disciples do not believe the report of the two travelers on Emmaus road, but Luke does not comment on the initial belief or unbelief because Jesus appears to the disciples while they are still talking about these appearances (Luke 24:36).

They gave him a piece of broiled fish, and he took it and ate before them.

JOHN 20:19-23

On the evening of that day, the first day of the week, the doors being locked where the disciples were for fear of the Jews, Jesus came and stood among them and said to them,

"Peace be with you."

When he had said this, he showed them his hands and his side. Then the disciples were glad when they saw the Lord. Jesus said to them again,

"Peace be with you.

As the Father has sent me, even so I am sending you."

And when he had said this, he breathed on them and said to them,

"Receive the Holy Spirit.

If you forgive the sins of any, they are forgiven them; if you withhold forgiveness from any, it is withheld."

COMMENTARY

On Sunday evening, the disciples gather together behind locked doors, hiding out of fear of the Jews.[31] The two disciples who had encountered Jesus on the road to Emmaus had recently arrived, and as they discuss the amazing occurrences of the day, Jesus suddenly appears in their midst and seeks to allay their fears by saying, "Peace to you!"[32] Despite Jesus's words, the disciples are naturally frightened and believe Jesus to be a spirit.[33] Jesus further assuages their fears by inviting them to examine and touch his hands and

---

[31] John 20:19.
[32] Luke 24:36; John 20:19. Jesus's sudden appearance inside a locked room may indicate that his resurrected body could walk through walls; if so, his body was physical but with supernatural properties in its glorified state. Alternatively, he could have supernaturally unlocked the door from the outside as happened for Peter in Acts 12:10.
[33] Luke 24:37, 41.

feet, demonstrating that he is flesh and blood and not a spirit.[34] He decisively demonstrates the solid reality of his resurrection body by asking for something to eat and consuming a piece of broiled fish.[35] This last proof finally convinces them, since ghosts were generally viewed to be incapable of eating solid food.

Once the disciples calm down enough to listen, Jesus again exhorts them to peace and gives the Johannine Great Commission: "As the Father has sent me, even so I am sending you."[36] As he commissions them, the risen Lord breathes on his followers, conveying the sense of imparting on them the Holy Spirit so they can fulfill their mission.[37] Jesus's next statement in John's account concerning the forgiveness of sins likely points to the church's proclamation of the gospel. In the gospel proclamation, those who believe in Jesus will find forgiveness of sins while those who reject the message will fail to do so and retain their guilt.

In Luke's presentation of Jesus's words, the evangelist intentionally compresses words spoken by Jesus over the following forty days. This intentional compression of Jesus's words is evidenced by comparing Luke 24:47–51 with Acts 1:3–9 and the hint in Luke 24:45 that Jesus "opened their minds to understand the Scriptures," a process that took place over the entire time period of his resurrection appearances. The words spoken in Luke 24:44–49 appear to have been spoken near the end of the forty days of his resurrection appearances before ascending near Bethany on the Mount of Olives. This is confirmed when Jesus's statement in Luke 24:49 ("But stay in the city until you are clothed with power from on high") is compared with Acts 1:3–4 ("He presented himself alive to them after his suffering by many proofs, appearing to them during forty days and speaking about the kingdom of God. And while staying with them he ordered them not to depart from Jerusalem but to wait for the promise of the Father"). If Jesus had indeed instructed his followers on that first Sunday evening not

---

[34] Luke 24:39–40; John 20:20.
[35] Luke 24:41–43.
[36] John 20:21–23.
[37] This would historically be enacted when the Holy Spirit came and was poured out at Pentecost (Acts 2).

to leave Jerusalem, this would have been a clear contradiction of the angel's and Jesus's earlier words to meet him in Galilee (Matt. 28:7, 10; Mark 16:7) and the later accounts of resurrection appearances in Galilee (Matt. 28:16–20; John 21:1–23). What is more, in Acts Luke places these words on Jesus's lips after the forty days of resurrection appearances. It seems that after the Feast of Unleavened Bread ended (after eight days according to John 20:26), the disciples followed Jesus's instructions and returned to Galilee for a time (twenty to thirty days) before regathering in Jerusalem for the feast of Pentecost just prior to Jesus's ascension.

EPILOGUE

LATER APPEARANCES OF JESUS
AND THE ASCENSION

Jesus Appears to the Eleven, Including Thomas (John 20:24-31)

In his account of the resurrected Jesus's appearance to his inner circle, John notes that Thomas, one of the Twelve, was not there that first Sunday evening.[1] When the disciples recount the events of the evening to Thomas, he refuses to believe and famously responds, "Unless I see in his hands the mark of the nails, and place my finger into the mark of the nails, and place my hand into his side, I will never believe."[2] Thomas will settle for nothing less than absolute empirical proof, and his skepticism has been shared by many throughout history. He had staked his life on the fact that Jesus was the Messiah (in fact, he had already witnessed one resurrection, that of Lazarus! [John 11:16]) and was not now going to be taken in by a hoax. Jesus had failed; he had died. They had been wrong about him—that ship had sailed. Thomas's test was based upon the fact that Roman crucifixion was thorough and lethal, so a living man with the marks of crucifixion would have been unheard of and would point to the strong probability of supernatural resurrection. Thomas's response also may indicate that he did not completely disbelieve the disciples' report but assumed that they had seen a ghost or immaterial spirit and not a true resurrected

---

[1] John 20:24.
[2] John 20:25.

body. His proposed test was designed to prove the solidity of Jesus's real (yet resurrected) body.

Thomas does not have long to wait. The next Sunday (eight days later, counting the first Sunday), the disciples are again hiding behind locked doors—this time with Thomas in their midst.[3] As before, Jesus appears in the room and allays their fears by stating, "Peace be with you."[4] He immediately turns to Thomas— indicating supernatural insight, since Jesus had not been physically present with the disciples when Thomas had expressed his doubts—and takes him up on his test: "Put your finger here, and see my hands; and put out your hand, and place it in my side. Do not disbelieve, but believe."[5] John does not explicitly state whether Thomas takes Jesus up on his offer (though one surmises he did not), but the outcome is complete and utter belief. Thomas confesses Jesus as his Lord and his God, acknowledging his authority and divinity.[6]

Jesus concludes this brief appearance by pronouncing a blessing upon all who believe in him without physically seeing him in his resurrected body.[7] This blessing includes all believers throughout history beyond the initial generation of eyewitnesses. John follows up this pronouncement with two interesting statements. First, Jesus did many other things in the presence of his disciples that were not written in the Gospel—space constraints (not to mention the cost of book production in the ancient world) forced John and the other Gospel authors to be selective.[8]

Second, John provides a clear purpose statement for his Gospel: "But these [signs] are written so that you may believe that Jesus is the Christ, the Son of God, and that by believing you may have life in his name."[9] John did not write as a neutral, unbiased

---

[3] John 20:26.
[4] John 20:26.
[5] John 20:27.
[6] John 20:28. In John's Gospel, Thomas's confession is part of an *inclusio* with John 1:1, opening and closing the Gospel narrative with parallel references to Jesus's deity.
[7] John 20:29. See also Peter's similar reference that applies to all believers today: "Though you have not seen him, you love him. Though you do not now see him, you believe in him and rejoice with joy that is inexpressable and filled with glory" (1 Pet. 1:8).
[8] John 20:30. See the similar statement in John 21:25.
[9] John 20:31.

observer but as someone who had been an eyewitness of the events described and who was passionately convinced of their truthfulness, believing that eternal life could be obtained only through faith in Jesus, the Son of God. He writes both to communicate information and to persuade readers and hearers to believe.

Jesus Appears to Some at the Sea of Galilee (John 21)

As observant Jews, the disciples remain in Jerusalem through the completion of the Festival of Unleavened Bread, which ended on Thursday.[10] Following the festival, many of the disciples follow the angel's and Jesus's instructions to return to Galilee. Among other reasons, Jesus may have directed his followers to Galilee in order to ensure that they understood that he had not come back to life in order to overthrow the Roman soldiers and Jewish leadership centered in Jerusalem. He was not seeking political dominance.

John does not indicate how long the disciples waited upon their return to Galilee but picks up the story one day with Peter, Thomas, Nathanael, the sons of Zebedee (James and John), and two other unnamed disciples. Peter, either hungry, bored, or out of money, announces that he is going to start fishing again.[11] Waiting for Messiah to appear did not pay the bills or put food on the table. The other six disciples present, following Peter's leadership, readily join him. They fish throughout the night—the preferred time to fish in the ancient world so that the fish could be sold fresh in the morning—but unfortunately fail to catch anything.

At dawn, Jesus calls to the distraught disciples from the shore, asking if they had caught anything. Like Mary Magdalene and the two disciples on the road to Emmaus, the disciples do not recognize Jesus, perhaps assuming he is a potential customer, and give him a short answer: "No."[12] Jesus instructs them to cast the net on the right side of the boat. They obey despite the fact that such

---

[10] See Matthew 26:17, which mentions Passover preparations on "the first day of Unleavened Bread." The Feast of Unleavened Bread fell on Nisan 15–21 (see also Lev. 23:5–6).
[11] John 21:3.
[12] John 21:5.

an act would naturally make no difference and proceed to catch so many fish they cannot pull the net into the boat. Upon seeing the great catch of fish, John (the beloved disciple) announces his belief that the man on shore is Jesus. In contrast to the hesitant and frightened Peter on the night of the crucifixion, Peter now expresses unbridled joy, immediately diving in and swimming ashore while the other disciples slowly drag the net to shore from the boat.

They find Jesus cooking fish over a charcoal fire, the same kind of fire around which Peter had denied Jesus.[13] After instructing Peter to help pull in the net full of 153 fish, Jesus invites the disciples to breakfast and gives them the bread and fish. The number 153 likely does not carry any symbolic significance but simply indicates the number of fish—fishermen counted their catch before selling it at market, and there is no indication that the disciples simply let all the fish rot on the beach. John relates that none of the disciples dare to ask Jesus who he is because they all know it is.[14]

After breakfast, Jesus officially reinstates Peter to service by asking him three times if he loves him and commanding him three times to feed or tend his lambs or sheep.[15] The thrice-repeated affirmation of love parallels the three earlier denials—a fact readily apparent to those present.[16] Jesus as the true shepherd recommissions Peter as a subordinate shepherd of God's flock (see Peter's account in 1 Peter 5:1–4). Jesus follows this up by predicting the kind of death—crucifixion—Peter will suffer ("glorify God") and by giving Peter a choice by commanding him to follow. Will Peter follow Jesus, knowing that it will certainly lead to his own crucifixion when he has just recently denied Jesus and failed to follow him in order to avoid possible death? Will Peter make good on

---

[13] John 21:9; see also 18:18.

[14] John 21:12.

[15] John 21:15–17. Popular suggestions to the contrary, the two different Greek words for "love" used in this passage (*phileō* and *agapaō*) do not likely carry any significant difference in meaning since they are often used interchangeably and since John often uses different words with similar meaning for stylistic variety.

[16] Earlier, Jesus had instructed Peter to strengthen his brothers upon Peter's repentance for denying his Lord (Luke 22:32).

his boisterous promise during the Last Supper that he will follow Jesus to the death?[17] Peter's earlier promise had been based upon his arrogance and self-reliance along with wrong expectations of the way God's Messiah would inaugurate his kingdom. The power motivating this later commitment comes from full awareness of his own weakness and frailty along with a greater understanding of the overwhelming power of Jesus's grace and forgiveness. He will indeed follow.

Peter turns and sees that John, the beloved disciple, has been following them as they had walked and talked, so he asks Jesus about John's fate. Peter is curious whether John will also have to die for Jesus. Jesus gently rebukes Peter—"If it is my will that he remain until I come, what is that to you? You follow me!"[18] Jesus thus reminds Peter that it does not matter what happens to others; he is responsible only for his own obedience and faithfulness. John inserts an editorial comment into the narrative at this point to clarify a confusion that had evidently arisen among some of Jesus's followers on the basis of Jesus's words. John informs the reader that Jesus's words did not indicate that John would avoid death but rather that John's fate was not Peter's business.

John concludes his Gospel with a personal eyewitness affirmation of the truthfulness of the words (see especially the phrase "I suppose," an epithet of authorial modesty)—and events described within it—along with a caveat concerning the necessary selectivity of his presentation.[19]

The Great Commission
(Matt. 28:16-20; Luke 24:45-49; John 20:21-23; Acts 1:8)

Matthew 28:18–20 contains what is commonly called the Great Commission. These are Jesus's last words recorded in Matthew's Gospel, although we know from the other Gospels and Acts that these were not Jesus's final words before his ascension. By end-

---

[17] John 13:36–38.
[18] John 21:22.
[19] John 21:24–25.

ing his Gospel with these words, Matthew draws attention to the importance and centrality of the commission—for Matthew, the Great Commission summed up Jesus's entire post-resurrection message.

Matthew provides some context for these important words. Following the Festival of Unleavened Bread, the eleven disciples travel to Galilee to a certain mountain in obedience to Jesus's instructions. Matthew notes that when Jesus appears to them, they worship him, but some continue to doubt.[20] There on that mountain Jesus communicates the earth-shaking results of his resurrection—Jesus now has all authority in heaven and on earth. As a result, his followers must now go out into the entire world to make disciples of all nations by baptizing them and teaching them everything that he has commanded. The central command of the commission is to make disciples, that is, to develop genuine, life-long followers of Jesus. Jesus's command to baptize "in the name of the Father and of the Son and of the Holy Spirit" points to a Trinitarian understanding of God and to the deity of Jesus. Jesus affirms his continued presence and empowerment until the end of the age.[21] His followers are not being called upon to embark on this mission alone. Jesus will be with them.[22]

Because of Jesus's resurrection, the message of God's kingdom is no longer to be limited to the Jewish nation but must be proclaimed to every nation and every person everywhere in the world.[23] Matthew makes clear that this is a direct command from Jesus, the resurrected king of the world, to his followers. The Great Commission is not a mere wish or suggestion; it is a command

---

[20] The reference to doubters may not refer to the eleven disciples. According to 1 Corinthians 15:6, Jesus also appeared to more than five hundred followers. If this appearance to more than five hundred corresponds to Matthew's description of Jesus's appearance on the mountain, it would be quite possible that some of the large group doubted, at least initially.

[21] Some believe that Jesus's reference to baptism "in the name of the Father and of the Son and of the Holy Spirit" is hopelessly anachronistic, since it reflects a clear Trinitarian understanding, which, they allege, is a mark of subsequent doctrinal formulation in the early church. However, there is no good reason to question the historicity of Matthew's account at this point, and the Gospels make clear that Jesus repeatedly referred to both God the Father and the Holy Spirit throughout the course of his ministry.

[22] He is God's Immanuel, "God with us" (Matt. 1:23).

[23] The Greek word *ethnē* refers not to nation-states but to people groups (i.e., every tribe, tongue, people, and nation).

that is just as valid and relevant for Jesus's followers today as it was when it was first given.[24]

Luke's version of the Great Commission is recorded in two places and was spoken near Jerusalem just prior to the ascension. The Lukan Great Commission states that "repentance and forgiveness of sins should be proclaimed in his name to all nations, beginning from Jerusalem. You are witnesses of these things" (Luke 24:47–48), accompanied by Jesus's promise that "you will receive power when the Holy Spirit has come upon you, and you will be my witnesses in Jerusalem and in all Judea and Samaria, and to the end of the earth" (Acts 1:8). Matthew's description of perpetual presence is repeated in Luke's account in terms of the supernatural empowerment of the Holy Spirit for the activity of witness to the entire world.

The Johannine Great Commission—"As the Father has sent me, even so I am sending you"—is followed by the symbolic impartation of the Spirit and a description of the forgiveness of sins that will accompany the church's proclamation of the gospel.[25] The followers of Jesus are sent by Jesus into the world just as God sent Jesus into the world. Jesus's followers share his mandate and mission and are empowered by the Spirit in their work.

The continual reappearance of the Great Commission motif using different words in different contexts indicates not that the individual Gospel authors mixed up Jesus's words but that the theme of the Great Commission is a major element of his post-resurrection teaching (Matt. 28:18–20; Luke 24:47–48; John 20:21–23; Acts 1:8), which goes on over a period of forty days (Acts 1:3). Jesus continually emphasizes it in different contexts and with different words. It is imperative that the disciples not miss this important command. They are to go into the entire world in the power of the Spirit, sent by Jesus as witnesses to his resurrection and his kingdom. The centrality of this element of Jesus's post-resurrection appearances must not be missed or downplayed.

---

[24] It is arbitrary to restrict one part of the commission as temporary where the other aspects— e.g., Jesus's authority and presence—are universal and eternal.
[25] John 20:21–23.

Being a Christian is defined in Jesus's post-resurrection teaching as obeying the Great Commission. It is the mandate that is to define the very existence of his followers.

The Ascension (Luke 24:50-53; Acts 1:9-11)

Luke alone records Jesus's ascension, not once but twice. Jesus had evidently directed his followers to return to Jerusalem early for Pentecost. Luke describes him as leading them out to the Mount of Olives overlooking Bethany.[26] Being back in Jerusalem, the disciples are naturally curious: will Jesus finally establish his earthly kingdom?[27] Jesus responds not by denying the reality that he will one day establish an earthly kingdom, but by emphasizing that it is not for his followers to know God's timing.[28] He then proceeds to issue the Lukan Great Commission to make clear, once again, what they should be doing while they wait for his return—they must actively bear witness to him throughout the entire world.

After giving this commission, Jesus blesses his followers and disappears upward into a cloud.[29] This should not be understood as a rain cloud high up in the atmosphere, as if Jesus were some kind of human rocket ship. A cloud is often associated throughout Scripture with God's presence.[30] Jesus is lifted up—Luke does not indicate how high—until he is enveloped by the cloud of God's presence. Luke records in his Gospel that the disciples worship Jesus, return to Jerusalem with joy, and continually bless God in the Jewish temple.[31] In the book of Acts, Luke records the additional information that two men in white robes—angels—speak with them and assure them that Jesus will return in the same way he left; he will descend in a visible, physical, resurrected body.[32]

---

[26] Luke 24:50; Acts 1:12.
[27] Acts 1:6.
[28] Acts 1:7.
[29] Luke 24:50–51; Acts 1:9.
[30] Exodus 13:21; 14:19–20; 19:9, 16; Luke 9:34–35.
[31] Luke 24:52–53.
[32] Acts 1:10–11. The apostle Paul writes that when Jesus returns, those who have believed will marvel at him—at his appearance (2 Thess. 1:10); and as the church regularly celebrates Communion, God's people proclaim Jesus's death until he comes (1 Cor. 11:23–25; see also Matt. 26:25–29 pars.).

WHO DO YOU SAY
THAT HE IS?

With this, the amazing story of Jesus comes to an end, at least as far as the Gospel witness is concerned. Jesus's "final days" were not the end, however. While his sinless life, substitutionary death, and triumphant resurrection accomplished our salvation, Jesus's work still continues. After he ascended to heaven and took his place at his Father's side, he sent the Holy Spirit to empower the church's gospel witness to the ends of the earth. Even now, he upholds the universe by his powerful word, intercedes for us with the Father, and is preparing a place for us in heaven. At one glorious future day, he will return to take us home with him. He will judge the unbelieving world, and the devil and his demons, and we will live with him in God's presence for all eternity.

Will you and I believe? Will we place our faith once and for all in the one who came and died and rose again so we can be forgiven and have eternal life? If so, our Easter has dawned, and God's Morning Star has arisen in our hearts.[1] For true believers, every day is Easter, and we can celebrate Easter joyfully, thanking God for his amazing salvation and looking forward expectantly to the day when our Lord will return and summon us to spend eternity with him, for his glory and for our eternal happiness.

"The Spirit and the Bride say, 'Come.' And let the one who

---

[1] See Revelation 22:16.

hears say, 'Come.' And let the one who is thirsty come; let the one who desires take the water of life without price. . . . He who testifies to these things says, 'Surely I am coming soon.' Amen. Come, Lord Jesus!"[2]

[2] Revelation 22:17, 20.

ACKNOWLEDGMENTS

Justin

I am thankful for Andreas, for his excellent scholarship, his love for the Lord, and his willingness to partner with me in producing this book. Under God, the three main spheres of my life and vocations are my family, my church, and my work. I am deeply grateful to God for my wife, Lea, and our three kids (Claira, Malachi, and Cecily); my fellow elders and the precious flock at New Covenant Bible Church; and my colleagues at Crossway (under the leadership of Lane Dennis), including Lydia Brownback, who lent her expertise to the editing of our manuscript. "The lines have fallen for me in pleasant places; indeed, I have a beautiful inheritance" (Ps. 16:6).

Andreas

I am grateful to Justin for suggesting to me the idea for this book and inviting me to partner with him to see it to completion. I am also grateful to Alexander Stewart, my research assistant, who did an excellent job in helping me prepare a serious first draft of the manuscript. As always, my wife, Marny, encouraged me to go ahead with this project because she was convinced that it is a much-needed resource for the church and for individual families. Your support means so much to me!

I continue to be grateful for the friendship and partnership of so many gifted and godly people at Crossway who do their job with excellence and distinction. Finally, I am grateful for my children who are now old enough to actively support and encourage their dad's writing ministry. You bring so much joy to my life! My prayers are with you as you go through high school and college and find your way in this often perplexing, fast-changing world. Remember that Jesus Christ is faithful, and he—and he alone—will *never* let you down:

> "I will never leave you nor forsake you." So we can confidently say,
>
> > "The Lord is my helper;
> > I will not fear;
> > > what can man do to me?" . . .
>
> Jesus Christ is the same yesterday and today and forever. (Heb. 13:5–6, 8)

SUGGESTIONS FOR FURTHER READING

Introductions to Jesus and the Gospels

BEGINNING

Alexander, T. D. *Discovering Jesus: Why Four Gospels to Portray One Person?* Wheaton, IL: Crossway, 2010.

INTERMEDIATE

Blomberg, Craig L. *Jesus and the Gospels: An Introduction and Survey*. 2nd ed. Nashville: Broadman, 2009.

Bock, Darrell L. *Jesus according to Scripture: Restoring the Portrait from the Gospels*. Grand Rapids, MI: Baker, 2002.

Pennington, Jonathan T. *Reading the Gospels Wisely: A Narrative and Theological Introduction*. Grand Rapids, MI: Baker, 2012.

Strauss, Mark L. *Four Portraits, One Jesus: An Introduction to Jesus and the Gospels*. Grand Rapids, MI: Zondervan, 2007.

ADVANCED

Keener, Craig S. *The Historical Jesus of the Gospels*. Grand Rapids, MI: Eerdmans, 2009.

Historical Reliability of the Gospels

Bauckham, Richard. *Jesus and the Eyewitnesses: The Gospels as Eyewitness Testimony*. Grand Rapids, MI: Eerdmans, 2008.

Blomberg, Craig L. *The Historical Reliability of the Gospels*. 2nd ed. Downers Grove, IL: IVP Academic, 2007.

————. *The Historical Reliability of John's Gospel: Issues and Commentary*. Downers Grove, IL: IVP Academic, 2001.

Harmonizing the Gospels

Cox, Steven L., and Kendell H. Easley, eds. *Harmony of the Gospels*. Nashville: Broadman, 2007 (2nd ed. forthcoming).

Knight, George W. *A Simplified Harmony of the Gospels: Using the Text of the HCSB*. Nashville: Broadman, 2000.

Poythress, Vern Sheridan. *Inerrancy and the Gospels: A God-Centered Approach to the Challenges of Harmonization*. Wheaton, IL: Crossway, 2012.

Steinmann, Andrew E. *From Abraham to Paul: A Biblical Chronology*. Saint Louis: Concordia, 2011 (chaps. 11–13).

Wenham, John. *Easter Enigma: Are the Resurrection Accounts in Conflict?* 2nd ed. Grand Rapids, MI: Baker, 1992.

The Passion and Resurrection

BEGINNING

Strobel, Lee. *The Case for Easter: A Journalist Investigates the Evidence for the Resurrection*. Grand Rapids, MI: Zondervan, 2004.

INTERMEDIATE

Evans, Craig, and N. T. Wright. *Jesus, The Final Days: What Really Happened*. Louisville: Westminster, 2009.

Kiehl, Erich H. *The Passion of Our Lord*. Eugene, OR: Wipf & Stock, 2002.

Stott, John R. W. *The Cross of Christ*. Downers Grove, IL: InterVarsity, 2006.

ADVANCED

Chapman, David W., and Eckhard J. Schnabel. *The Trial and Crucifixion of Jesus: Texts and Commentary*. Tübingen: Mohr Siebeck, forthcoming.

Wright, N. T. *The Resurrection of the Son of God*. Christian Origins and the Question of God, vol. 3. Minneapolis: Fortress, 2003.

Commentaries and Reference Works

Bock, Darrell L. *Luke*. Baker Exegetical Commentary on the New Testament. 2 vols. Grand Rapids, MI: Baker Academic, 1994, 1996.

Green, Joel B., Jeannine K. Brown, and Nicholas Perrin, eds. *Dictionary of Jesus and the Gospels: A Compendium of Contemporary Biblical Scholarship* 2nd ed. Downers Grove, IL: InterVarsity, 2013.

Köstenberger, Andreas J. *John.* Baker Exegetical Commentary on the New Testament. Grand Rapids, MI: Baker Academic, 2004.

Stein, Robert H. *Mark.* Baker Exegetical Commentary on the New Testament. Grand Rapids, MI: Baker Academic, 2008.

Turner, David L. *Matthew.* Baker Exegetical Commentary on the New Testament. Grand Rapids, MI: Baker Academic, 2008.

Wilkins, Michael, Craig Evans, Darrell Bock, and Andreas Köstenberger. *The Holman Apologetics Commentary on the Bible: The Gospels and Acts.* Nashville: Broadman, 2013.

Introductions to the New Testament

BEGINNING

Towns, Elmer L., and Ben Gutierrez, eds. *The Essence of the New Testament: A Survey.* Nashville: B&H Academic, 2012.

INTERMEDIATE

Köstenberger, Andreas J., and L. Scott Kellum, and Charles L. Quarles. *The Lion and the Lamb: New Testament Essentials from* The Cradle, the Cross, and the Crown. Nashville: B&H Academic, 2012.

ADVANCED

Köstenberger, Andreas J., L. Scott Kellum, and Charles L. Quarles. *The Cradle, the Cross, and the Crown: An Introduction to the New Testament.* Nashville: B&H Academic, 2009.

GLOSSARY AND REFERENCE GUIDE

Annas. The patriarchal former high priest who presided over the initial hearing of Jesus (John 18:12–24; see also Luke 3:2). His official rule was from AD 6 to 15, and he was succeeded by his son-in-law Joseph Caiaphas. While the Romans were the ones who appointed and deposed high priests, the Jews considered the position to last for life. The power of Annas's Sadducee family is seen in the fact that his successors after Caiaphas included five of his sons. He died in AD 35, two years after Jesus's execution. His headquarters may have been a two-story palatial mansion on the eastern slope of the Upper City (the Jewish Quarter of the Old City of Jerusalem), just southwest of the Temple Mount.

Arimathea. See *Joseph of Arimathea.*

Barabbas. A prisoner released by Pilate as a Passover custom. *Bar-abbas* is an Aramaic patronymic meaning "son of the father," and an early scribal tradition identifies his name as "Jesus Barabbas"—which would add to the irony of his release instead of Jesus the son of the eternal Father. All of our information about Barabbas comes from the Gospel accounts. He is characterized as a notorious revolutionary (Matt. 27:16), guilty of murder and plunder during an insurrection in Jerusalem (Mark 15:7; Luke 23:19, 25; John 18:40). He may have had supporters in the crowd (see Mark 15:18), and the two thieves on the cross may have been arrested for similar crimes.

Battalion. At full strength this would be six hundred Roman soldiers (also known as a "cohort"), one-tenth the size of a "legion." They gathered before Jesus at Pilate's headquarters (Matt. 27:27; Mark 15:16).

Beloved Disciple. The apostle John's self-designation in his Gospel, which identifies the author (21:24–25; see also 21:20) as an eyewitness to

Jesus's Last Supper in the upper room (13:23), his crucifixion (19:35), and the empty tomb (20:8).

Bethany. A village about 2 miles (3.2 km) east of Jerusalem where Jesus resided the last week of his earthly life. He likely lodged in the home of his friends Lazarus, Mary, and Martha.

Caiaphas, Joseph. A son-in-law of Annas and the acting high priest who presided over Jesus's Jewish trial. A Sadducee, he ruled nineteen years (AD 18 to 36), longer than any other high priest in the first century (high priests were often deposed after a year in office). It was Caiaphas who offered a political prediction during the plot to kill Jesus that John interprets with deeper theological meaning and irony (John 11:49–52; see also 18:14). The Caiaphas Ossuary (bone box), which may well be authentic, was discovered in South Jerusalem in 1990. Now another ossuary has been found of Caiaphas's granddaughter, with Caiaphas spelled the same slightly unusual way in Hebrew.

Calvary. Latin equivalent of *Golgotha* (see below).

Centurion. A skilled Roman officer in command of a century (up to one hundred, but usually between sixty and eighty soldiers). After the crucifixion and the earthquake, the centurion at Golgotha praised God, acknowledged Jesus's innocence, and confessed Jesus as the Son of God (Matt. 27:54; Mark 15:39; Luke 23:47); he also confirmed to Pilate that Jesus was dead (Mark 15:44–45).

Cleopas. One of two disciples of Jesus who encountered the risen Messiah on the road to Emmaus (Luke 24:13–35). Cleopas was likely with either his wife or a friend.

Crucifixion. Crucifixion is a deliberately painful method of execution in which a condemned person is tied or nailed to a wooden cross and left to hang until dead. This Roman way of executing criminals, often for rebellion against Rome, was looked at with horror by the Jews. It was considered equivalent to being hanged on a tree, a shameful death for those cursed by God (Deut. 21:23; see also Gal. 3:13).

Day of Preparation of the Passover. Friday, the day before the special Sabbath of Passover week (John 19:14, 31, 42).

Emmaus. A town about 7 miles (11 km) northwest of Jerusalem. It was on the road to Emmaus that the resurrected Jesus revealed himself to two of his followers (Luke 24:13–35). It likely took a couple of hours to walk this distance.

Farewell Discourse. See *Upper Room.*

Feast of Unleavened Bread. A weeklong festival (Nisan 15–21) commemorating Israel's deliverance from Egypt, celebrated in Jerusalem after Passover (Nisan 14–15). The two events (Passover and the Feast of Unleavened Bread) were treated as one. In AD 33, the festival was from April 3–9, with Passover on April 2–3.

Gethsemane. Aramaic for "oil press," this garden (perhaps enclosed with a wall) was located at the foot of the western slope of the Mount of Olives, about 300 yards (or 274 m) east/northeast of Jerusalem and the Temple Mount.

Golgotha. Aramaic for "the skull," this hill outside Jerusalem was where Jesus and two thieves were crucified. It was likely a quarry to the west of Jerusalem's Second Wall and near the Gennath (Garden) Gate, allowing those visiting the city for Passover to observe the spectacle. The Vulgate, a fourth-century Latin translation of the Bible, uses the equivalent term "Calvary." Its likely location today is at the Church of the Holy Sepulchre.

Greeks. God-fearing Gentiles (including, but not limited to, actual Greeks). They had come to Jerusalem to worship at the Jewish festival.

Hasmonean Palace. Herod Antipas's luxurious home in Jerusalem where part of Jesus's Roman trial was conducted. Herod Antipas lived there during his reign, from 4 BC to AD 39. His father, Herod the Great— who sought to eliminate Jesus at his birth—lived there from the mid-30s to 23 BC while he waited for Herod's palace to be built.

Herod Antipas. One of Herod the Great's four sons, he was a ruler in Galilee and Perea who inherited part of his father's kingdom upon his death in 4 BC. He reigned for forty-two years, from 4 BC to AD 39. He was known as "Herod the Tetrarch" [i.e., ruler of a quarter].

Herod's Palace. The fortress in Jerusalem that served as the headquarters and residence of Pontius Pilate when he visited from Caesarea Maritima. Herod the Great had the palace built, and he lived there from 23 to 4 BC. It was presumably here that Herod the Great received the Magi and then plotted to kill the infant Jesus (Matt. 2:1–18). It is also the likely location of Jesus's final condemnation under Pilate.

High Priest. A powerful position usually held by Sadducees. Appointed by the Roman governor, the high priest served as president of the Sanhedrin, collected taxes, supervised the temple, and represented Jewish interests before Rome.

Joanna. Among the first women to discover the empty tomb (Luke 24:10), she was the wife of Chuza, the household manager or steward of King

Herod Antipas. She was a follower of Jesus and helped to provide financially for Jesus's ministry, along with Susanna and many others (Luke 8:3).

John. See *Beloved Disciple*.

Joseph of Arimathea. A Pharisee who was a secret disciple but feared what fellow Jews would think of him if they knew his allegiance (John 19:38). He was wealthy (see Matt. 27:57), was a respected member of the Sanhedrin who did not agree with the Council's treatment of Jesus (see Luke 23:50–51), and was originally from the Jewish town of Arimathea (Luke 23:50). Joseph requested possession of Jesus's body from Pilate and was granted permission to bury him in a newly hewn rock tomb that he owned near a garden and near Golgotha (John 19:41).

Judas Iscariot. One of Jesus's twelve original disciples, he served as the treasurer, was known to steal money from their collective moneybag (John 12:6), and was the son of Simon Iscariot. He betrayed Jesus with a kiss for the price of thirty pieces of silver, and then hung himself after Jesus was condemned to die (Matt. 27:1–10; see also Acts 1:18–19).

Judgment Seat. The Greek word *bēma* indicates a raised area used for official judgments (John 19:13; see also Matt. 27:19). See also *Praetorium*.

Kidron. A valley or ravine running along the eastern side of Jerusalem. After the Last Supper, Jesus and his disciples crossed it to enter the garden of Gethsemane. John 18:1 refers to it as "the brook Kidron," indicating that there was an intermittent stream running through the valley during the rainy season.

Last Supper. Jesus's final meal with the Twelve, a Passover meal, where he instituted the new covenant (Matt. 26:17–29 pars.; John 13:1–2, 26–28). See also *Passover*.

Legion. A Roman army unit composed of nine cohorts and one first cohort (5,120 legionaries plus a large number of camp followers, servants, and slaves). Including the auxiliaries, it could contain as many as six thousand fighting men. Jesus reminded Peter that his Father could send more than twelve legions of angels (i.e., over 60,000) to intervene for him (Matt. 26:53).

Lord's Day. The early church started worshiping on "the first day of the week" (John 20:1), the day Jesus rose from the dead, rather than on the Sabbath, calling that first day of the week "the Lord's Day" (Rev. 1:10).

Malchus. A bondservant of the high priest Caiaphas. His right ear was cut off by Peter and immediately healed by Jesus during the arrest (John

18:10; see also Matt. 26:51; Mark 14:47). One of Malchus's relatives, a fellow bondservant of the high priest, questioned Peter about his relationship with Jesus (John 18:26).

Mary Magdalene. A Galilean woman probably from the town of Magdala (on the west bank of the Sea of Galilee). Jesus delivered her from seven demons (Luke 8:2; Mark 16:9). She became a follower of Jesus (Matt. 27:57), a witness to the crucifixion and burial (Matt. 27:61; 28:1; Mark 15:40, 47; John 19:25), and was among the women who went to the tomb on Sunday (Mark 16:1; John 20:1). She was the first person to see Jesus alive (Mark 16:9) and told the other disciples (Luke 24:10; John 20:18).

Mary (mother of Jesus). She gave birth to Jesus, raised him, was present at his execution and burial, and witnessed his resurrection life. From the cross Jesus entrusted his widowed mother to John's care, and she went to live in his home (John 19:25–27)—perhaps because Mary's other sons were not yet believers (John 7:5; see also Matt. 13:57; Mark 3:21, 31; 6:4). Mary's other sons were named James (author of the biblical book of James), Joseph/Joses, Simon, Judas/Jude (author of the biblical book of Jude) (Matt. 13:55; Mark 6:2–3; Acts 1:14; 1 Cor. 9:4–5; Gal. 1:19). She also had at least two daughters (Mark 6:3).

Mary (mother of James and Joses/Joseph). A witness of Jesus's crucifixion, burial, and resurrection appearances. Her sons were named James the Younger (hence her husband must have been named James) and Joses/Joseph. See Matt. 27:61; 27:56; Mark 15:40, 47. The fact that two Marys in the story have sons with the same names (James and Joseph/ Joses) shows the commonality of certain surnames in first-century Galilee. The name Mary, in particular, was exceedingly common in first-century Palestine, hence the need to distinguish between different Marys in the Gospels, whether by way of their hometown (Mary Magdalene) or in association with their husband (Mary of Clopas) or sons (Mary mother of James and Joses).

Mary (sister of Martha and Lazarus). Jesus's friend from Bethany who hosted Jesus during the last week of his earthly life in the home she shared with her siblings Lazarus and Martha (Luke 10:38–42; John 11:1–2; 12:1–8). She anointed Jesus's head with oil (Matt. 26:6–13; Mark 14:3–9; John 12:1–8; but not Luke 7:36–50, which features another, earlier anointing of Jesus by a "sinful woman").

Mary (wife of Clopas). A Galilean witness of Jesus's crucifixion, she may be identified as Jesus's "mother's sister" (John 19:25)—though see discussion under *Salome* below. According to Hegesippus, as quoted by the historian Eusebius, Clopas was the brother of Joseph of Nazareth (*Hist. Eccl.* 3.11; 3.32.6; 4.22.4). If so, Mary and Clopas were Jesus's aunt and uncle. Their son Simeon (Jesus's cousin) became a leader of the Jerusalem church succeeding James the brother of Jesus.

Mount of Olives. A mountain ridge east of Jerusalem, named for its olive groves. It was a "Sabbath day's journey away" from Jerusalem—i.e., about 1,100 yards or 3/5 of a mile. The garden of Gethsemane lay at the foot of the slope. The Mount of Olives was the site of Jesus's end-time discourse (also called "Olivet Discourse"; see also Matt. 24:3 pars.) and his ascension (Acts 1:12).

Nicodemus. A Galilean Pharisee and member of the Sanhedrin who had a substantial conversation at night with Jesus on the new birth (John 3:1–15), pled with his fellow Jewish leaders for fairness regarding Jesus (John 7:50), and brought a substantial aromatic mixture of spices to preserve the corpse of Jesus (John 19:35).

Nisan. A month spanning March and/or April in the Jewish calendar.

Passover. Celebrated annually in Jerusalem to remember God's deliverance of Israel from Egypt. Passover began on Nisan 14–15 (April 2–3 in AD 33).

Peter. See *Simon Peter*.

Pilate, Pontius. A Roman citizen, a member of the equestrian (middle) class, and the Roman governor of Judea and Roman prefect under Emperor Tiberius. He ruled from AD 26 to 36. He ruled over all non-Roman citizens in Judea and Samaria. His headquarters and residence were in Caesarea Maritima, about 68 miles (110 km) northwest of Jerusalem. Pilate was in Jerusalem for Passover in AD 33, staying in his Jerusalem headquarters, the former palace of Herod the Great (see *Herod's Palace*).

Praetorium. Pilate's official headquarters in Jerusalem, a fortress within Herod's palace. A raised Stone Pavement (Aramaic *Gabbatha*) was the place of official judgments (see Matt. 27:27; Mark 15:16; John 18:28, 33; 19:9).

Sabbath. The Jewish day of worship and rest, which began at sundown on Friday night and went until Saturday evening.

Salome. One of Jesus's female followers in Galilee, she witnessed the crucifixion and went to the tomb on Sunday (Mark 15:40; 16:1). The parallel passage in Matthew 27:56 makes it likely that she is the mother of the sons of Zebedee (i.e., James and John). Interpreters differ on the number of women represented in the Greek construction in John 19:25 ("his mother and his mother's sister, Mary the wife of Clopas, and Mary Magdalene"). If "his mother's sister" is a separate woman, the reference is likely to Salome (which would make James and John the cousins of Jesus). However, it seems slightly more likely that Mary the wife of Clopas is Mary's sister (or sister-in-law). See the discussion under *Mary (wife of Clopas)*.

Sanhedrin. Or "Council." Headquartered in Jerusalem and comprised of both Pharisees and Sadducees, this was the highest ecclesiastical court of the Jews and the highest national body in charge of Jewish affairs. At full strength it may have had seventy elders, but twenty-three members present were sufficient for a quorum. The president of the Council at the time of Jesus's arrest was Caiaphas the high priest.

Simon (of Cyrene). An African man, likely a Jew, from Cyrene (a region in North Africa with a large Jewish population) who carried Jesus's cross to the site of the crucifixion on Golgotha. Simon and his sons Alexander and Rufus were likely traveling to Jerusalem for Passover. The mention of his sons' names may indicate that they were believers in the early church.

Simon Peter. Spokesman for the Twelve (e.g., John 6:68–69), paired with the "beloved disciple" in the second half of John's Gospel (e.g., 21:15–23), who denied Jesus three times prior to the crucifixion (18:15–18, 25–27) but was subsequently reinstated into service by Jesus (21:15–19).

Twelve, the. Jesus's twelve core disciples (Matt. 10:1–4 pars.): Simon Peter and Andrew (brothers), James and John (brothers, sons of Zebedee), Philip, Bartholomew (Nathanael), Thomas, Matthew (Levi), James (son of Alphaeus), Thaddaeus (Judas the son of James), Simon (the Zealot), and Judas Iscariot (son of Simon).

Unleavened Bread, Feast of. See *Feast of Unleavened Bread*.

Upper Room. The location of the Last Supper and of the Upper Room (or Farewell) Discourse (John 13–16). Most peasant houses in Jerusalem were small, with two levels but only one room. By contrast, this room was large and on the second level, indicating that the owner of the house was a person of means. It may or may not be the same location as the disciples' headquarters prior to Pentecost (Acts 1:13).

DOWNLOAD A FREE STUDY GUIDE AT
crossway.org/finaldaysguide